HAUNTED SOUTHERN NEVADA GHOST TOWNS

HAUNTED SOUTHERN NEVADA GHOST TOWNS

HEATHER LEIGH, PHD

FOREWORD BY CHRIS MCKINNELL
DIRECTOR OF THE WARREN LEGACY FOUNDATION FOR PARANORMAL RESEARCH

Published by Haunted America
A Division of The History Press
Charleston, SC
www.historypress.com

All images by the author unless otherwise noted.

First published 2022

Manufactured in the United States

ISBN 9781467151504

Library of Congress Control Number: 2022936605

Notice: The information in this book is true and complete to the best of our knowledge. It is offered without guarantee on the part of the author or The History Press. The author and The History Press disclaim all liability in connection with the use of this book.

I am dedicating this book to my husband, Josh, and son, Aidan, who tag along with me on my crazy ghost adventures. Without your support, I do not believe this book would have been possible. I also dedicate this book to my parents, Michael and Nancy, who never once discouraged me from researching the paranormal. And, of course, to Liam, who has always been a cherished part of my life.

Finally, I cannot forget to mention my grandfather, Archie Geeraerts, whose spirit set my journey into paranormal research rolling. Thank you, grandpa, for putting me on a path filled with many unique adventures.

I also want to dedicate this book to all the miners, frontiersmen, business owners and the women who made southern Nevada what it is today.

CONTENTS

FOREWORD

As the director of The Warren Legacy Foundation for Paranormal Research and the grandson of Ed and Lorraine Warren, famously portrayed in the movies *The Conjuring* and *Annabelle*, as well as a host of books, I have witnessed many strange types of phenomena in my more than forty years exploring the paranormal around the world. I began working with my grandparents when I was sixteen, back in 1980. I worked alongside them or led investigations on some of their most famous cases, including the Haunting in Connecticut (spending nine and a half weeks with the Snedeker family in a haunted old funeral home), the Haunted (the Schmurls of West Pittston, Pennsylvania) and the tragic case of Maurice Theriault, documented in the book *Satan's Harvest*. My entire life, I have studied the supernatural and its links to psychology and quantum physics, from the United States to the Sahara, the Himalayas to the Amazon, England to Israel. Every region in the world has different ways these spirits and energies manifest. It is a fascinating window into our power in shaping our local reality, both in life and after death.

The Warren Legacy Foundation for Paranormal Research is a nondenominational worldwide organization that continues my grandparents' work that began in 1952. This global network of professional researchers includes doctors, psychologists, priests and bishops, as well as witches, Taoists and others from all walks of life. We help people who believe they are afflicted by the paranormal and educate the public and the next generation of paranormal researchers. Our services are offered freely and anonymously to all who ask. Most times, the activity can be explained away as natural phenomena, but about 10 percent of the time, something is going on that science struggles to explain. Luckily, we have an outstanding, dedicated network of professionals worldwide ready to help.

One of those people is our head administrator, Dr. Heather Leigh Carroll-Landon. She is a fantastic researcher who meticulously uncovers hidden details of our cases to help our clients get the services they need. She is also an extraordinary teacher who shares her decades of knowledge in a straightforward and easy-to-understand manner. You are fortunate to have found this book. There is so much ridiculous misinformation on all media platforms today. Whether it be movies, TV, books or YouTube, the information there is usually false or very misleading. Heather Leigh is different. She has a strong desire to educate others so they can truly understand this bizarre world we live in and be perhaps less afraid when they let go of their ignorance. I have had the pleasure of working closely with Heather Leigh for quite some time and know her to be one of the best researchers in the world.

I was very touched when she asked me to write the foreword for this tour of the haunted ghost towns of southern Nevada. I thoroughly enjoyed learning more about this region of the world and the spirits that populate this desolate landscape. With a blend of history, storytelling and simply laid out theory, Heather Leigh brings these places to "life" and broadens our knowledge of what is possible after we die as well. There are so many mysteries and unusual occurrences that science can't yet explain, but they are a part of our world. Heather Leigh helps us understand this hidden world quite a bit better.

I am eagerly awaiting whatever she writes about next. I hope you enjoy this exploration of an area world-renowned for its haunting and haunted landscape as much as I have.

—Chris McKinnell
Director of The Warren Legacy Foundation for Paranormal Research

Acknowledgements

Writing this book was a bit more challenging than I expected. Though I have explored the towns included in this book, I didn't realize there were many more personal paranormal experience stories out there, and I did not take as many photos as I thought I did. Of course, none of this would have been made possible without the help of fellow paranormal researchers, local historians and many others.

The trouble with being a paranormal researcher is that not everyone wants to hear ghost stories, talk about haunted locations or go into strange places for investigations. However, I am truly blessed to have an understanding husband, Joshua Landon, and son, Aidan Carroll-Landon, who not only talk about ghostly experiences but help in my research. They are even brave enough to venture off into unknown places to investigate and experience the paranormal firsthand.

I am eternally grateful for Chris McKinnell, director of The Warren Legacy Foundation for Paranormal Research, not only for his beautiful foreword but also for helping me fine-tune my paranormal research skills. He has taken me under his wing and has been an excellent resource for my ongoing research. I also love teaching others by his side and look forward to the many great things we will accomplish for the foundation.

Working in the paranormal field is not easy, and several of my fellow paranormal researchers have helped with research and making this book possible. Thank you, Brian J. Rollins, co-founder of SisBro Paranormal in Nevada, for allowing me to use some of his amazing photos of southern

Nevada ghost towns and for sharing his experiences with me. You will see his pictures and stories throughout this book. Also, Brian Williamson has been a great supporter of my research and is always willing to lend a helping hand when needed. You will find many stories about his personal experiences scattered throughout this book as well.

When it comes to the history of Goldfield, Nevada, there is no person more knowledgeable than Jon Aurich, owner of the Florence Mine. He has a wide range of knowledge about the area, mining operations and the people who developed and shaped the town into what it is today. He invited other researchers and me to be the first paranormal team to investigate the Florence Mine. You will find several of those stories in this book. Thank you, Jon, for being so supportive of the paranormal field and sharing information about the history of the Florence Mine and the city of Goldfield.

One of the most unique places I have ever visited was the International Car Forest of the Last Church in Goldfield, Nevada. It was such an impressive display of creativity and had a small hidden gem paranormal researchers find intriguing. I want to thank Sharon Artlip, president of the International Car Forest of the Last Church, for sharing details about this location and allowing me to use one of her photos in this book.

Additionally, I want to thank Ryan MacMichael for allowing me to use his excellent photos of the Boulder City Pet Cemetery and thank him for maintaining a fantastic website honoring those buried in the cemetery.

The true inspiration for writing this book came when the producers of Motion Picture Video asked me, my husband and my son (our paranormal team, Exploration Paranormal) to appear in the filming of *Real Haunts: Ghost Towns* and *Real Haunts 3*. During the filming, we explored the history of southern Nevada ghost towns, such as Goldfield, Gold Point and Nelson, which inspired me to write down our experiences and adventures. All of that information evolved and grew into what you will find in this book. Thank you, Brett Gerking and Gina Watson, for including us in this fantastic project.

One of my favorite locations in southern Nevada is not a ghost town but represents the local mining industry. The McCaw School of Mines offers opportunities to learn about mining operations and history in Nevada. The museum, the staff and the volunteers have so much knowledge and make visiting a cherished experience. I am grateful that Cindy Liberatore, mine manager, and Phil Luna, executive director, put up with my quirkiness and allowed us to conduct paranormal investigations at their location. They are a true treasure to have in southern Nevada and a must-experience for anyone looking to learn more about mining.

Finally, I want to thank The History Press for allowing this first-time author to share my knowledge and stories about the ghosts I and many others have encountered in southern Nevada. In addition, a huge thank-you goes out to Laurie Krill, my acquisitions editor, for being patient with me and very helpful in answering all of my questions during this exciting journey.

INTRODUCTION

Have you ever visited a location and felt like you were not alone? That feeling is exactly what happens when you explore one of southern Nevada's ghost towns. Many of these towns have the spirits of former residents lingering in the shadows, waiting to engage with visitors and explorers. Since these ghosts live where very few people come through, it is easy to believe why many people have paranormal encounters in ghost towns. The ghostly residents look for people to interact with and make themselves known.

Southern Nevada is a unique place to visit and contains endless desert landscapes. In addition, the Silver State is home to several ghost towns, which were once just as active as significant cities of today. These towns boomed in the late nineteenth and early twentieth centuries, providing a reason for those on the East Coast of the United States and in other countries worldwide to make their way to the Western Front.

However, like a bouncing ball, what goes up, must come down. Many boomtowns hit their peak and quickly fell like that bouncing ball. As mines closed, several residents left behind all their belongings, searching for a better life. Some ghost towns still have residents working, maintaining and preserving local history, while others became entirely abandoned. One town included in this book survived, and I have included some of the spooky stories surrounding this working ghost town.

Many of these towns are not as abandoned as we would like to think. The spirits of those who created these boomtowns still reside, going about their business, creating spooky experiences for those who dare to visit. Ghost towns are like our own Disneyland for paranormal researchers, and we get very excited to explore these areas.

I wrote this book for my love of paranormal research and the joy I had from investigating many of the ghost towns in southern Nevada. Plus, I love to share my knowledge and experiences with others. Put all of that together, and you have *Haunted Southern Nevada Ghost Towns.*

I sincerely hope you enjoy this book as much as I have enjoyed researching and writing it. My goal was to help others better understand these ghost towns, their history and the paranormal activity. I also wanted to demonstrate that there is nothing to fear regarding the paranormal activity manifesting in southern Nevada ghost towns. I hope other paranormal researchers use this book as a guide to finding places to investigate and experience paranormal activity.

Please note that when exploring southern Nevada ghost towns, remember not to break the law and never trespass on private properties. Additionally, remember the Boy Scout policy for outdoor exploration ethics: "Leave No Trace." When visiting a ghost town, do not leave trash behind, do not destroy property and leave it as it was when you arrived. The only thing that should be left behind is your footprints from walking in the dirt. Finally, do not remove anything from a location. Leave everything as it was so others can enjoy and explore the site as you have.

One final note. Do not go alone when visiting ghost towns or conducting a paranormal investigation. Not exploring alone is for your safety because you never know what can happen or who or what you might encounter. Plus, it is more fun to explore and investigate with a buddy anyway.

Are all of the ghost stories in this book true? Many are, while many others are unconfirmed experiences of other paranormal researchers and urban legends. However, that does not mean the stories are not valid. The many experiences, stories and legends are some of the best things about the paranormal field of study. We take urban legends and personal experiences of others and use them as a platform to jump off for continued experiments, investigation and research—all in the hope of proving the paranormal exists and why and how it exists.

With all of that said, I hope you enjoy learning about ghost towns, especially those found in southern Nevada.

CHAPTER 1

WHAT MAKES A GHOST TOWN?

Nevada has a unique history haunted by many memories of the past. Outside of the major cities, such as Las Vegas, Henderson, Reno and Carson City, most of the state has vast open desert lands sprinkled with booming Western Front remnants. Today, these towns sit abandoned or near abandoned. In the past, ghost towns were booming cities, several having the largest populations in the state and all of the West. These towns were growing fast, and everyone wanted to be part of the development, establishment and creation of these mining towns and major cities in the late 1800s and early 1900s.

Settlers worldwide traveled to Nevada in search of riches, especially as more and more gold, silver, lead and other precious metals came pouring out of the hills and mountains. Almost every day, miners and residents made discoveries, and word of more mining opportunities quickly spread across the country. Word of mining opportunities encouraged more people to trek westward, giving up the life they knew to search for their fame and fortune.

As the population of these towns quickly boomed, the current resources and amenities were not enough to support the city's infrastructure and its residents. Ultimately, each of these towns had to adapt swiftly, and it did not take long for several saloons, newspapers, hotels, stores, restaurants, schools and brothels to pop up. All of these businesses contributed to the rapidly growing economy of Nevada.

However, as World War I began, workforce efforts needed to be focused elsewhere. Many young men went off to war, and human resources on the

Street scene from Goldfield, Nevada, around 1907. *Library of Congress.*

homefront required reallocating to make weapons to help the United States win the war. Additionally, the price of gold and silver dropped drastically during this time, causing less of a need to search for new precious mineral deposits. With prices so low, it was near impossible to compensate mine owners, prospectors and miners for the costs associated with operating a mine. These reasons were the main contributing factors to many mining operations ceasing by the 1920s.

As a result, mining was no longer a way of life for many as they were encouraged to pursue other employment or business endeavors.

As mines closed throughout the state, several residents in towns such as Nelson, Goldfield and Gold Point started to move away. With jobs disappearing as fast as gold had appeared in the state, residents seemed to have vanished from their hometowns with what little they could carry with them. As a result, buildings were abandoned, businesses were shuttered and the streets became near silent. The rapid departure of residents in search of employment elsewhere turned many of these historic towns into what are known today as ghost towns.

Some of the towns are considered working ghost towns, which means there are still a few residents living there, working, playing and supporting the local economy the best they can. Goldfield is one example of a working ghost town in Nevada. Other ghost towns, such as Gold Point and Nelson, have been completely deserted, only purchased by those wanting to live quiet lives and help restore Nevada's mining history.

So what exactly is a ghost town? By definition, according to the Oxford English Dictionary,[1] a ghost town is a "deserted town with few or no remaining inhabitants." Essentially, a ghost town is any town, village or city that has been nearly deserted or wholly deserted by the community's

Right: Remnants of an abandoned mine in Goldfield. *Library of Congress.*

Below: View from within the mill house at the Florence Mine in Goldfield.

residents. In many cases, when residents vacate a town, they leave behind evidence of a once-booming economy. Remnants of buildings and infrastructure are still visible in many of Nevada's ghost towns. Several ghost towns were plagued with natural and human-caused disasters at one point in history, such as extended droughts, fires, war, government misuse of resources or floods. For many, the uncontrolled lawlessness the Wild West is known for significantly contributed to the fall of these towns. Once jobs were lost, there was no reason to continue living in a lawless city, and to save their own lives, residents moved away, leaving the gunslingers behind to control the town.

Another significant event causing financial distress for southern Nevada mining towns was the financial panic of 1907. This event put a damper on mining operations, and many residents and employees also paid the price of the economic fallout following the 1906 earthquake in San Francisco.[2] The only saving grace many mining towns had during the crisis was the continued flow of silver from the mines. Unfortunately, World War I caused many primary mining operations to cease.

During this time, the sheriff was many towns away, and in some cases, such as with Nelson, it was several hours before the sheriff would arrive. In many cases, if there was no death involved, residents didn't even call the sheriff, and in other cases, he didn't bother to respond when called to these lawless communities.

Over time, businesses came and went as industries expanded west through Nevada. Railroad companies, entrepreneurs and others seeking fame and fortune continued to move west through Nevada, causing an ebb and flow of financial success and disaster.

Luckily, southern Nevada was resurrected thanks to the United States military on December 18, 1950, establishing the Nevada Testing Site (NTS). The NTS covered a 680-mile section of the Nellis Air Force Base and Bombing Grounds authorized by President Harry Truman.[3] The site helps experiment with, test and develop various weapons, including nuclear weapons for the National Nuclear Security Administration.

Visiting some ghost towns in Nevada is like stepping back in time, especially when visiting communities that worked to restore and preserve the city precisely the way it was when it was a booming mining town. Some of these preserved towns look like they did in the late 1800s and early 1900s, with many original buildings still standing. Other ghost towns have been fully or partially restored, with several original buildings still there. Some communities have added to the original buildings or made significant repairs, while other historical buildings have been relocated and new buildings erected.

Museums throughout the state have worked hard to preserve historic buildings and homes from ghost towns. Several restoration projects, historic landmark dedications and the relocation of buildings have helped preserve the history and keep the memory of these once-thriving communities alive.

One example is the Clark County Museum in Henderson, Nevada. This museum houses many relocated buildings from ghost towns, including the

The Giles-Barcus House as it sits on Heritage Street at the Clark County Museum in Henderson, Nevada.

Giles-Barcus House. This cottage home, initially located in Goldfield before being relocated to Las Vegas, was built in 1924 by Edwin Schofield Giles. He moved from Colorado to Goldfield in 1907 with his wife, Edith Corlissand, and their daughter, Edith.[4] After living in a wagon, tent, several hotels and other houses, the family acquired the twenty-six-foot by twenty-four-foot cottage in 1928.

Their daughter, Edith Giles Barcus, moved to Las Vegas in 1955 and could not leave her childhood home behind. She relocated the house to the corner of Hacienda and Giles Streets in Las Vegas, where it became an antique shop called the Odd Shop. Upon her death in 1991, she donated it to the museum, and it opened to the public in 1992.

Like many other ghost town buildings, several reports of paranormal activity occurred in the Giles-Barcus House, with some believing it could be caused by the original owners. No official statements regarding paranormal activity have been made, nor has any substantial evidence been collected; however, many have shared stories about feeling watched, being touched, hearing footsteps and seeing unexplained shadows when in the building.

Unfortunately, many more ghost towns in Nevada have been forgotten or left to ruins. Remnants of the original buildings come up from the sand and are overrun by vegetation and wildlife. Though these once lively towns have been forgotten, they are exciting places to explore and learn about the history of the Silver State.

Many ghost towns throughout Nevada allow you to walk along paths where many once walked the streets, and some of the original residents may tag along for your ghost town exploration.

CHAPTER 2

WHY ARE GHOST TOWNS HAUNTED?

Ghost towns are a hotbed for paranormal activity, allowing supernatural entities, spirits and residual energy to linger once the living have moved on. Everything from death to mayhem and destruction to high energy levels contributes to paranormal activity in a location. During their boom, southern Nevada ghost towns had high levels of energy flowing through the streets, in businesses and within private residences. In addition, countless fights, accidents and diseases left many dead, causing high levels of emotional swings among the town's residents.

Energy is everywhere, and ghost towns present a historical setting with happy and sad emotions. Both tragic and exhilarating events have contributed to the high levels of energy that remain today in many of southern Nevada's ghost towns. This energy, mixed with the emotions and energy of those living in these towns, helps fuel paranormal activity, making these towns unique places to explore, visit, research and investigate.

Ghost towns have many antiques and older items with paranormal energy attached. Whether it is weapons, furniture, statues, jewelry, toys or pictures, many older things carry energy imprints and spirit attachments from previous owners, the environment and tragic events occurring near the object. These items have been left undisturbed and hidden among the rubble of declining ghost towns. Many more reside in chambers of commerce, historical society buildings, antique shops and museums. The energy held in these objects can contribute to the paranormal activity experienced when near them.

Objects belonging to Douglass Dressner are now on display at McCaw School of Mines in Henderson.

In some cases, spirits are not attached to the object. Instead, they remain behind after their deaths to protect their property. For example, many ghost town spirits stay behind to defend their claims, property and homes. Even when these items no longer exist, the spirits remain, living life as if they were back in the 1800s and early 1900s.

One myth is that a death has to occur in a location for it to be haunted. That idea is furthest from the truth. Though many haunted places result from death, it is not a requirement for paranormal activity to occur. Death in a home, building, neighborhood or anywhere else in a ghost town could be one reason these towns remain haunted. Especially when the death was violent or sudden, the spirit could linger because it does not know it is dead or is seeking retribution for its death.

In the event of sudden death, the spirits may not know they are dead and continue with life as they knew it. Sudden death and accidents are why so many mines are full of ghosts who continue to work. For example, when a mine collapses, the miners often may not know what has happened. As a result, they continue with their daily mining activities. In other cases, the

hostile intentions and inexperienced users can open portals and attract the wrong spirits. Once the spirits are invited in, the investigators leave, thinking everything is okay. However, in reality, the spirit or negative entity does not leave once the ritual has ended, even if you ask it nicely.

There have been many reports of hostile paranormal activity, including some demonic reports, in ghost towns with rumors of ill-intentioned individuals conducting these rituals. Plus, these locations are abandoned, making them the perfect backdrop for these rituals, with little to no interference from law enforcement or locals disturbing them.

Another theory behind why ghost towns are haunted is because we are told they are haunted. Story after story claiming to experience something supernatural in a rundown building leads our minds to believe a natural occurrence to be paranormal. Additionally, the power of self-manifestation can create and cause paranormal activity to occur around us. When we are told time and time again a location is haunted, eventually, the spirits we are told reside there manifest, officially haunting the place. Could the paranormal activity in a ghost town be a manifestation of our remembering and reliving history? Could era cues and reenactments help with the manifestation of paranormal activity? It is all very possible.

So is the paranormal activity we experience a glimpse into the past or something we have manifested ourselves? Only time will tell, and that is for an entirely different book. This book contains the stories shared about paranormal activity experienced in the many haunted ghost towns in southern Nevada.

So why are not all ghost towns haunted?

Though ghost towns offer the perfect environment for paranormal activity to thrive, not all towns have ghosts. Nevertheless, ghost towns may not have paranormal activity for several reasons:

- There may be no reports of paranormal activity, or no one wants to report their experiences.
- The current residents may be so wrapped up in their own lives they do not notice the activity surrounding them.
- Some ghost towns did not have high happy or sad emotional energy levels, ultimately not leaving a paranormal imprint in the area.

The Tommy-Knockers

Did you know that paranormal activity has been experienced in mines worldwide, including southern Nevada, since mining operations began? Tommy-Knockers have been blamed for haunting mines for hundreds of years. Are these entities serving as a warning for miners in dangerous conditions, or are the mischievous beings there to cause trouble?

The profession of being a miner is an ancient way of earning a living. As long as miners have been working underground, the legend of the Tommy-Knockers has been passed around mining camps. These underground creatures are most notable for causing all sorts of chaos in the mines underneath the surface of the earth.[5]

Every region around the world has its own image of a Tommy-Knocker. For example, the Cornish equivalent of Irish leprechauns or the English brownies are gnome-like creatures (typically men) who linger within the walls of these underground mines. The Cornish believed that these creatures were the souls of Jewish men who crucified Christ and were sent as enslaved people to work in the tin mines by the Romans. The intent behind this belief was so strong that Tommy-Knockers in this culture never manifested on Saturdays or Jewish holidays.

Then you have the Germans, who called them Berggeister, which means mountain ghosts or little miners. Most saw Tommy-Knockers as two-foot-tall creatures with a greenish tint to their skin. They looked like men, wearing traditional miner's attire, but were a percentage of the size and very naughty. Every legend has the Tommy-Knockers doing good and bad things to the miners working.

In southern Nevada, Tommy-Knockers were spirits or entities that looked like miners who were there to cause chaos or protect the workers. For centuries, it was believed that if you heard the knocks or whistles of the Tommy-Knocker, the mine was about to collapse. These knocks were a sign for the miners to get out of the mine. When the miners had made it to safety, the mine they had just escaped from collapsed.

Are the knocks heard in the mines caused by Tommy-Knockers? Or is it the wood starting to give way before the mine collapses? Either way, the knocks were a warning and saved the lives of many miners. Regardless of the cause, many miners believed the sound of the Tommy-Knockers was a sign of imminent death, and it was time to get out of the mine.

In addition to doing good, some people believed that the Tommy-Knockers caused many of the mines to collapse. It was almost a daily occurrence that miners would experience tools missing or strange occurrences throughout the workday. They typically would blame these mischievous acts on the Tommy-Knockers. Some things that happened included unattended tools and food going missing, candles getting blown out or small touches or pushes while working in the mines.

The legend of the Tommy-Knockers is a common story when exploring southern Nevada ghost towns, and these tiny creatures may be the cause of some of the paranormal activity happening just beneath the surface of many former mining camps in the Old West.

CHAPTER 3
BEATTY, BULLFROG AND RHYOLITE

I n a far-off, distant land in southern Nevada, paranormal explorers and history fanatics can find the communities of Beatty, Bullfrog and Rhyolite. These communities are located within a volcanic rock canyon, nestled on the rim of Death Valley. Beatty is now a small town, with several businesses still in operation today, including gas stations, hotels and restaurants. Bullfrog and Rhyolite are actual examples of ghost towns, and all that is left behind are the remnants of former residents. With such a beautiful landscape, unique landmarks and historic buildings, it is no wonder why Rhyolite is one of the most photographed Nevada ghost towns. Millions of visitors travel to the area to experience an authentic southern Nevada ghost town.

The areas of Beatty, Bullfrog and Rhyolite were booming during the gold rush, but like many others, these towns declined in population as quickly as they boomed. Each of these communities contains a lot of history and several reports of paranormal activity. The booming city of Rhyolite had more than ten thousand people living, working and playing within it. Like Beatty and Bullfrog, Rhyolite has had several reports of paranormal activity, and other oddities remain, including a home built out of beer, whiskey and medical glass bottles.

Rhyolite's origins began in 1904, when Shorty Harris and Ernest L. Cross traveled through the area prospecting for silver and gold.[6] Word of their discovery spread like wildfire throughout the region, and in a short time, the population rose to several thousand. Shortly after, Old

Left: A tourist stands in front of a building in Rhyolite. *Library of Congress.*

Below: The remains of an old school building in Rhyolite. *Brian J. Rollins.*

Man Beatty, who lived on a ranch five miles away, was joined by many who rushed to the area to set up several mining camps as part of the Bullfrog Mining District. Quickly, more than two thousand mining claims covered the thirty-mile area within the Bullfrog Mining District, bringing the community to a quick boom, with buildings popping up everywhere, including shops, a miners' union hospital, schools, ice plants, two electric plants in 1907, homes, saloons, banks and brothels.

Like in many other nearby towns, in the 1920s, mining operations slowed within the Bullfrog Mining District. The shuttering of many mines caused

The historic railcar sits alone in the desert in Rhyolite. *Brian J. Rollins.*

Buildings like this one remain standing in Rhyolite, Nevada. *Brian J. Rollins.*

the ultimate collapse of the area. Today, some buildings remain, including remnants of the bank buildings, general store and train depot.

These communities had many residents living there, going about their everyday lives, and then suddenly, one day, everything and everyone vanished. If it were not for reports of mining operations ceasing and businesses shutting down, it would have seemed as if everyone mysteriously disappeared. However, as with the many other ghost towns in southern Nevada, residents needed to find a way to survive. The unfortunate demise of their precious communities forced them to seek residence and employment elsewhere.

Paranormal experiences throughout the area include seeing apparitions of former residents, hearing eerie footsteps and being touched. In addition, hundreds of explorers and visitors to these communities have claimed to have heard voices echoing through the streets, mines and decaying structures. Several reports also claim to have seen shadow figures roaming the streets, peering out of windows and dashing through the cemetery.

THE BOTTLE HOUSE

In 1905, Tom T. Kelly built what is known as the Bottle House.[7] This home is a true oddity and a must-see when exploring the area. Kelly used close to fifty thousand beer, whiskey, liquor, champagne and glass medicine bottles, gathered over the course of six months from the many saloons in the area, to build his home.[8] The Bottle House in Rhyolite is the oldest and largest home

A tourist is photographed while visiting the Bottle House in Rhyolite. *Library of Congress.*

of its kind in the world. Paramount Pictures restored the home in 1925 with a new roof to prepare it for filming a movie.

Given how much sweat Kelly put into creating his three-bedroom home, he and other residents of Rhyolite might haunt the area. Though there are no reports of paranormal activity in the house, there are several reports of activity throughout Rhyolite, including in nearby buildings and locations found in this chapter.

Goldwell Open Air Museum

On a lonely road leading to Death Valley, California, sits a uniquely magnificent outdoor museum that is home to ghostly displays and several artistic creations. The Goldwell Open Air Museum was created by a group of Belgian artists led by Albert Szukalski. This art exhibit features seven colossal sculptures towering over the upper Mojave Desert, including a ghostly interpretation of the *Last Supper* by Leonardo da Vinci,[9] a pink woman made from cinder blocks standing twenty-five feet high, a blossoming statue of gleaming chrome parts and a winged woman statue. The museum also has a twenty-four-foot-tall steel prospector accompanying a penguin representing Shorty Harris's story about seeing a penguin while experiencing a whiskey hallucination.

This fifteen-acre outdoor sculpture park is home to more than the unique art installations. Several reports have been made of paranormal activity and ghostly sightings throughout the entire open-air museum. One account is from a Google Earth photo[10] showing two figures with glowing eyes looking up through open sewer sluice gates. Could these red eyes be something paranormal, or could they be an animal catching and reflecting the moonlight in its eyes?

Other paranormal reports from those who have investigated the Goldwell Open Air Museum include seeing shadow figures near the ghostly *Last Supper* display, spotting full-bodied apparitions and seeing darting light anomalies dance around the various art displays. In addition, many who have visited this ghost town attraction have reported eerie feelings, sounds of ghostly footsteps and the sensation of being watched.

The Bullfrog-Rhyolite Cemetery

The Bullfrog-Rhyolite Cemetery is littered with graves made out of rocks in the shape of human bodies. Unfortunately, few markers or tombstones remain to signify who is buried in the cemetery. The lack of information about those laid to rest in the town's cemetery adds to the eeriness of the surrounding area. Those who visit must use their imaginations when thinking about who is buried there, but chances are many of the graves are filled with former residents from Rhyolite, Bullfrog and Beatty.

Reports of paranormal activity in the cemetery include hearing disembodied voices, boot-covered footsteps and strange, unexplainable sounds. In addition, many paranormal investigators have reported seeing strange light anomalies and light orbs. These anomalies and orbs have been spotted with the naked eye and are not to be confused with dust particles or insects seen in videos or still photographs.

A fenced grave found at the Bullfrog-Rhyolite Cemetery. *Brian J. Rollins.*

Above: Grave marker at the Bullfrog-Rhyolite Cemetery. *Brian J. Rollins.*

Left: A view of the Bullfrog-Rhyolite Cemetery. *Library of Congress.*

ANGEL'S LADIES BROTHEL

Nevada is a prostitution-friendly state, and one of the popular things to do when visiting Beatty was to stop by one of the many area brothels. Angel's Ladies Brothel[11] cannot be missed when traveling to Beatty from Las Vegas. This roadside attraction has a crashed twin-engine plane, a bright pink sign promising all-night truck parking and beautiful ladies.

Though many visited the brothel for a good time, the site was not all about happy times. At one point, there was a promotion offering anyone who could parachute out of a plane and land on a mattress in a large painted star a naughty prize. The lucky winner would receive a night with the lady of their choice for free. Unfortunately, one day, an inexperienced pilot distracted by scantily clad women got caught up in crosswinds and crashed the brothel's promotional plane. No one was injured in the accident; however, the promotion ended, and the wreckage remains on site today.

The brothel closed in August 2014, and the structure is falling into disrepair. In addition to the plane wreckage, the abandoned brothel structure remains but presents an eerie sensation when approaching the building. Several visitors have stopped by to see this Nevada landmark and see if they can capture a glimpse of former prostitutes from back in the day or other Beatty residents lingering in the desert.

THE BROWN MAN

Every ghost town has a tragic story of death, and the legend of the Brown Man is Rhyolite's murderous ghost story. It is said that a prospector brought huge gold nuggets to town to be tested. Unfortunately, he was poisoned by the town's barber, who wanted his gold. Today, there are reports of seeing a brown shadow with a giant floppy hat, like many prospectors wore back in the day, wandering the streets of Rhyolite.

The Rhyolite Train Depot is another abandoned building in Rhyolite. *Brian J. Rollins.*

Like other Rhyolite buildings, the John S. Cook building crumbles, showing very little of the original building. *Brian J. Rollins.*

Another view of the collapsing John S. Cook building in Rhyolite. *Brian J. Rollins.*

Another claim is that people have seen an older man leading a mule pulling a cart full of gold mining equipment. This apparition appears out of nowhere, walks down the street and then vanishes as suddenly as he appears. Is this the same spirit as the Brown Man? It is uncertain, but they are seen in the same areas of town, and both appear to have been gold prospectors.

THE MONTGOMERY–SHOSHONE MINE

Set in Rhyolite, the Montgomery-Shoshone Mine[12] became famous in 1904 when prospectors made claims regarding the discovery of gold and silver. According to one of the original prospectors, Bob Montgomery, the mine produced approximately $10,000 in ore per day. Charles Schwab purchased the mine for millions of dollars in 1906, and it closed permanently in 1911. Today, the mine is surrounded by the few structures still standing in Rhyolite, where many have heard eerie sounds and spotted strange light anomalies in the area near the mine.

Could this be the activity of former miners? Or could Montgomery be lingering to ensure his claim is safe and secure? Unfortunately, the source of the paranormal activity remains unknown because there is very little information about paranormal activity in the mine itself, and no one has shared any significant evidence, claims or personal experiences regarding the Montgomery-Shoshone Mine.

CHAPTER 4

BELMONT

Though there are no consistent or accurate reports or claims of paranormal activity in Belmont, Nevada, this ghost town deserves recognition and inclusion in this book. Belmont is one of the most iconic ghost towns in southern Nevada and was once the second-largest city in the state with a population of more than fifteen thousand people. Many of the historic buildings still stand today and are very well preserved, which makes this town worth mentioning in this book.

Nestled not too far from the official Geographic Center of the State marker, Belmont was the county seat for Nye County back when it was booming. The landscape is speckled with stamp mill ruins and offers visitors sixty miles of vantage points to look out over the valley below.

Belmont is home to a one-hundred-foot chimney that was used in the 1940s by pilots from the nearby Tonopah Air Base during World War II for target practice. The airbase was one of the largest World War II training bases, and many of the pilots would venture to Belmont to use several of the community's chimneys as target practice. Today, the structure still has .40-caliber bullet holes in it. Additionally, the remains left behind from former residents include a bank, miners' cabins, abandoned mine shafts and the Belmont Courthouse.

This once bustling community is now a historic city with vacant buildings and tumbleweeds rolling down the streets. In 1865, the town experienced a significant boom after a silver strike, and by the 1870s, the town's population reached more than two thousand residents.[13] During its peak, the town had four stores, five restaurants, a school, a blacksmith shop and a bank. Today, Belmont is off the grid but offers paranormal explorers many opportunities to visit, explore, shop at the antique and jewelry shops and possibly encounter one of the original inhabitants.

Additionally, there are stories that Belmont used to be the location of a Manson family hideout. When officials were searching for Manson family victims, Charles Manson was hiding in Belmont, leaving behind a haunting clue for everyone to see at the Nye County Courthouse. On the first-floor door frame, Manson carved a small section of graffiti into the wood. The graffiti served as a reminder to all residents that Manson and his disciples hid out in Death Valley. The graffiti inscription reads, "Charlie Manson + Family 1969."

One part of this story not commonly known is how Rose Walter, the town's unofficial guardian for most of her ninety-three years of life, was responsible for sending the Manson family packing.[14]

Since the Manson family was in Belmont, the Nye County Courthouse has had many strange occurrences, including full-bodied apparitions, loud banging noises and floating light anomalies. Some paranormal researchers believe the paranormal activity could be associated with the victims of the Manson family. Additionally, some feel uncomfortable when exploring this secluded hideout. However, it could also be possible that Rose Walter continues to watch over Belmont, protecting the courthouse by making her presence known.

One day, Rose encountered a small group of people, including several young women, who wanted to camp in the town. Essentially, this was impossible because Rose had two rules: do not remove or take anything from the town and do not camp within the town's limits. Many who knew her said she had no fear or problem enforcing her rules and commanded respect.

When the Manson family was allegedly in Belmont, Rose would have been in her seventies. She told the group they could not stay in the town and pointed them toward a campground up the road with an authoritative voice. The group complied and moved their camp outside town. Reportedly, the group returned to town the next day to thank Rose for the campground location and said they were returning home to their ranch in Death Valley.

After some time had passed, while Rose was visiting a relative in another town, she saw a newspaper with a story about the Manson family and the crimes they allegedly had committed. In addition, the article shared photos of some of the members, whom Rose recognized as being part of the group she ran out of Belmont.

This is the story Rose told friends and historians who have tried to confirm the Manson family visit. However, there is no evidential proof, and anyone could have done the carving in the courthouse. Her personality and desire to protect Belmont lead many to believe she could have taken on one of the most infamous groups in American criminal history.

Visiting and exploring Belmont offers paranormal researchers access to many interesting buildings with finely crafted designs that are more than 150 years old. It is remarkable that these structures are in such good condition; many ghost towns have only tiny remnants of buildings that used to stand in the town. In this ghost town, several remaining miner cabins and mill sites provide the perfect environment for paranormal activity to occur.

Could the former residents still inhabit the community with the town preserved so well? Of course. The area is prime for those with an open mind to experience paranormal activity. Especially when visiting the old Belmont Courthouse, there is a chance of running into the spirit of someone from the Manson family or one of their victims.

CHAPTER 5
BOULDER CITY

T hough not a ghost town, Boulder City has a unique history and reports of many paranormal events. This town may not be an official ghost town, but the population is considerably less than when the Hoover Dam was under construction. The people and activity in the city put Boulder City just above being classified as a working ghost town while still being a thriving community just outside Las Vegas, Nevada.

BOULDER CITY PET CEMETERY

The first location to mention is the Boulder City Pet Cemetery, which is in a desolate area along the highway to Nelson from Las Vegas. The cemetery is set on the south side of U.S. 95 between Boulder City and Searchlight. It holds a fascinating history and is home to many beloved pets. The Boulder City Pet Cemetery is also the final resting place for the son of the famous Rin Tin Tin IV, Flash. It is rumored that this location was a popular dead body dumping ground for the mob, which could be true because it is in the middle of nowhere, with nothing around.

Initially, the pet cemetery was established on federal land but was not operated or managed by the government. Today, the land is owned by Boulder City. It was never legal to bury any remains—pet or human—on this land; however, many ignored the warnings and posted signs and buried

The Boulder City Pet Cemetery is home to many of the remains of beloved pets from the community. *Ryan MacMichael.*

their pets there anyway. Luckily, the remains of the illegally buried pets remain undisturbed today.

Many rumors are shared about how the Boulder City Pet Cemetery started. Back in the 1930s, it was rumored that several people started burying their beloved pets in an expansive area in the Nevada desert just south of Las Vegas. Another story involves Emory Lockette, who wanted to make some money and offered plots of land in the desert in the 1950s for pet owners to lay their fur babies to rest.[15]

Veterinarian Marwood Doud is another name often shared when discussing the start of the location where hundreds of people have buried their dogs and cats. It is believed he may have had a hand in helping develop this area by unofficially encouraging his clients to bury their pets there.

Those who have visited the cemetery have reported and shared stories about paranormal experiences. Common experiences include hearing strange sounds, being touched and seeing full-bodied apparitions of both people and pets. Several shadow figures have also been reported darting through the cemetery, quickly dashing from grave to grave.

One famous story is about the spirit of a lingering white cat that has been seen and felt rubbing at visitors' ankles, especially if she likes them. Many

Three crosses pay tribute to pets at the Boulder City Pet Cemetery. *Ryan MacMichael.*

have claimed to hear the jingle of bells, similar to that of a cat collar or a leash. Is this cat watching over the cemetery, or is it one of the pets buried there? No one knows the origin of this cat, but several have shared similar stories and experiences with this phantom feline.

Some pet memorials are adorned with simple crosses with the names scribbled in ink. Other monuments are more elaborate and complex, including decorations, chiseled headstones and fences. The rough, primitive graves give an eerie feeling when walking around the cemetery. The weird feeling and reports of paranormal activity are why many claim the Boulder City Pet Cemetery is one of the most haunted pet cemeteries globally.

Railroad Tunnels

The second haunted location in Boulder City includes a series of sites known as the railroad tunnels. These tunnels were created to allow easy

Top: The railroad tunnels once served as access for transportation of supplies to the construction site of the Hoover Dam. *Library of Congress.*

Bottom: Another view of the railroad tunnels that served as a means of supply transportation to and from the construction site of the Hoover Dam. *Library of Congress.*

transportation of supplies to the Hoover Dam during its construction. There have been several reports of paranormal activity, which is thought to be caused by the many men who lost their lives during the dam's construction.

OLD BOULDER CITY HOSPITAL

Forever missing from Boulder City's landscape is the Old Boulder City Hospital, which was believed to be one of the most haunted locations in the community. The hospital sat on top of a hill overlooking Lake Mead.[16] Constructed during the Great Depression to treat Hoover Dam workers and their families, this hospital eventually became a community center in 2012. When the community center opened, locals quickly discovered they were not alone when in the building. Several accounts of moaning and other explained noises, such as footsteps, whispers and knocks, were reported throughout the building. Many also reported spotting a few shadow figures and apparitions lurking in the corners of the center.

The Bureau of Reclamation reports that ninety-six deaths occurred during the construction of the Hoover Dam.[17] These are "official" deaths reported. Deaths occurred from drowning, falling rocks or slides, blasting, falls, being struck by heavy equipment and trucking accidents. These are just a few of the reports associated with the deaths among construction workers. All workers were sent to the Old Boulder City Hospital for treatment, including many who were rumored to have become ill from carbon monoxide poisoning from working within the dam's structure.

With so much death and devastation experienced by the families who lost loved ones, it is no wonder that this location was haunted.

BOULDER DAM HOTEL

It is nearly impossible to miss the Boulder Dam Hotel, a historic structure built in 1933, when exploring downtown Boulder City. This historic Colonial-style structure was once a popular destination for Hollywood's elite and international dignitaries, including Howard Hughes. Hughes spent time recovering at the hotel after his plane crashed into Lake Mead in 1943. The hotel remains open today, welcoming guests worldwide to stay when visiting southern Nevada. This hotel, designed by Henry Smith, is listed in the National Register of Historic Places.

The hotel also welcomes guests in the afterlife to remain, as there have been several reports of paranormal experiences within the hotel's walls. In 2021, *Vegas News* listed the Boulder Dam Hotel as one of the most haunted locations in the Vegas Valley. Paranormal activity includes hearing voices, being touched and other reports that may not be suitable for visitors who are faint of heart.

A popular paranormal account shared by many investigators is that of a former employee who reported hearing sounds of laughing, talking and music coming from the ballroom and the restaurant.[18] When the employee heard these sounds, both rooms were closed, and upon investigation to see what was causing the unexplainable sounds and disembodied voices, they found that no one was in the rooms. The same employee reported experiencing sounds of running water when walking by one of the bathrooms. Upon entering the bathroom, he discovered that none of the faucets were on, and everything appeared normal. However, upon leaving the bathroom, the door quickly slammed shut behind him.

Other reports of paranormal occurrences include smelling cigar smoke waft by and then disappearing as quickly as it appeared and the elevator doors opening for no reason in the basement. The list of paranormal experiences shared by others includes feelings of heaviness in the lobby, an unpleasant feeling, the sensation of hands on the shoulders when no one else is there, the sense of ankles being grabbed by unseen hands coming up from the floor and seeing partial apparitions. The rooms where the most activity occurs are 209 and 219. No paranormal investigations are allowed in the hotel, and employees are instructed not to discuss their paranormal experiences with others, which makes it challenging to confirm any paranormal accounts.

Some paranormal researchers believe the urban legend that night clerk Tommy Thompson still performs his duties in the hotel. Many have reported seeing his apparition appear in the library, walking down the hallway and in other areas he frequented when in the hotel.

Hoover Dam

The Hoover Dam is a prime location for paranormal activity, and many have reported encountering spirits and experiencing strange occurrences there. Several paranormal reports include seeing ghosts walking the dam or the Mike O'Callaghan–Pat Tillman Bridge and seeing shadows and hearing voices and footsteps in the tunnels within the dam. In addition, apparitions of men in period construction clothing have been spotted in the hallways and tunnels within the dam's structure, which is seventy stories tall and 660 feet thick.

Many who visit the Hoover Dam and take the behind-the-scenes tour experience various types of paranormal activity. The most common reports include hearing voices in the halls and being touched on the shoulder.

The construction of the Hoover Dam was a huge undertaking, with a lot of sweat and tears of those involved.

Other unexplainable experiences include sudden temperature drops in the hallways of the dam, flickering lights and sounds of water dripping when everything is tightly sealed up. Workers and visitors have reported hearing footsteps echoing in the corridors of the power plant area of the dam. Additionally, many workers have reported tools missing, equipment being tampered with and unexplainable equipment malfunctions. Because of the workers' experiences, many speculate that the Hoover Dam is one of the most haunted locations in the region.

Several rumors that continue to spread like wildfire involve the theory of bodies buried in the dam's cement. Though it makes for a good ghost story and would explain some of the paranormal activity, this is an urban legend; there are no bodies interred in the walls of the Hoover Dam. Instead, the dam was made using pre-constructed interlocking blocks assembled by puddlers who stamped and vibrated the blocks into place. So there was no possibility of workers falling into the concrete and drowning, as the legend suggests.

There are some reports that some of the ninety-six official deaths associated with the dam's construction were caused by drowning in the waters of Lake Mead. In addition, there are other reports of people who died near the dam in the waters of Lake Mead. These deaths include those who jumped to their death from the Mike O'Callaghan–Pat Tillman Memorial Bridge and plane crashes.

A look at the interior of the Hoover Dam where footsteps and disembodied voices are often heard.

It is believed that more than one hundred people have jumped to their deaths from the Hoover Dam, including a handful of people who jumped from the bridge overhead.[19] Several visitors have reported seeing the apparitions of jumpers reliving their final moments by appearing late at night, walking across the bridge and jumping into the Colorado River. In addition, several apparitions have been reported in areas where the public is not allowed after hours.

Though many have died in proximity to the Hoover Dam, there have been a couple of well-known plane crashes in the waters of Lake Mead. One plane crash resulted in the deaths of two people, and the other, still very tragic and emotional, ended in the survival of the entire crew.

Howard Hughes was an accomplished pilot and known for many aircraft innovations. However, no amount of training could prepare him for what was about to happen on May 16, 1943, when he was testing a new military seaplane.[20] The experimental seaplane suddenly nosedived, crash landing into the waters of Lake Mead. The impact of the water landing caused one propeller to snap off, and it ripped through the fuselage. Hughes barely made it out of the plane, surviving the crash; however, his two fellow passengers were not so lucky.

Mechanic Richard Felt was struck in the head by the snapped propeller. An inspector for the Civil Aeronautics Administration, William "Ceco" Cline, was knocked out of the plane into the lake. Hughes managed to

The Mike O'Callaghan–Pat Tillman Memorial Bridge is where many spirits are seen walking.

The Colorado River flows out to Lake Mead, where many plane accidents have occurred.

The Hoover Dam is home to many spirits who haunt the interior and exterior of the structure.

escape the aircraft with his co-pilot, Felt, and one other engineer before the aircraft sank to the bottom of the lake. Cline's body was never recovered. Felt died two days later in the hospital from his injuries.

Could the spirits of Cline and Felt roam the areas surrounding the waters of Lake Mead, searching for answers as to why their plane malfunctioned? It is possible, and being so close to the Hoover Dam, they could be among the many ghosts rumored to haunt the historical landmark.

It is also believed that high amounts of emotional energy can help encourage paranormal activity and imprint the environment. On the morning of July 21, 1948, a B-29 Superfortress traveled to the test area near Lake Mead for high-altitude atmospheric research.[21] After taking the final measurements, the pilot lowered the plane to what he and his co-pilot believed to be four hundred feet above the lake's surface. Reportedly, the altimeter was turned off (it is not known who turned it off), and at 230 miles per hour, the aircraft struck the water, sinking to the bottom of Lake Mead. Luckily, all the men—Captain Robert M. Madison, First Lieutenant Paul Hesler, Sergeant Frank A. Rico, Staff Sergeant David D. Burns and John W. Simeroth—survived the crash, watching the plane sink to the bottom of the lake from the safety of their life raft. To this day, the plane sits on the bottom of the lake. The underwater aircraft wreckage has been used as a tour site for divers.

People come from worldwide to experience an authentic Wild West adventure in Nelson. It is all about seeing living history. Nelson has quickly become a popular place to film movies, television shows and music videos. *Breakdown* with Kurt Russell was the first of many films and shows to be filmed in the area. This film was followed by *Eye of the Beholder* with Ashley Judd, Ewan McGregor and Jason Priestley in Nelson. Luke Bryant, Journey and David Blane have filmed music videos among Nelson's historic structures and artifacts.

An old piano sits outside in the desert sun and was where Donnie and Marie Osmond took album cover pictures. Beyonce also used the piano for music videos and photos.

There are even remnants of the filming of *3000 Miles to Graceland*,[25] which was filmed in 2001, starring Kurt Russell and Kevin Costner. The plane crash from the movie is still on display in the town, exactly where the production crew left it. The crashed plane adds to the creepiness of the town as you walk past several historical buildings and see the remnants of a plane crash, with its tail protruding up from the desert sands. Many people wonder if this was a military plane crash when in reality, the tail is a movie prop left behind by the production crew. The plane, crash site and surrounding debris were explicitly built for the movie.

The high emotions from the filming could help create paranormal activity, and who knows, maybe in the future, there will be apparitions from the shows, movies and other filmings that appear to paranormal researchers of the future.

Just past the tourist area of Nelson lie several abandoned cave systems. These caves are the remaining pieces of history left behind due to mining operations in Eldorado Canyon. The saddest thing about these caves is that they are so out of the way and are not being monitored. Because of the lack of supervision, history has been ruined by graffiti and trash left scattered around.

Since the owners of Nelson do not allow paranormal investigations in town or the Techatticup Mine, these caves provided an excellent backdrop for an investigation featured on *Real Haunts: Ghost Towns*. There is a lot of speculation about who could be haunting these caves, but the paranormal activity made for some interesting experiences. Could the spirits lingering in these caves be those of Civil War soldiers who were labeled as deserters? Or could it be the Native American, Avote, who murdered four people, including Nelson, after whom the town was named? These are just theories based on the community's history but are the best possible answers to who haunts Nelson and Eldorado.

Above: One of the many beautifully restored buildings in Nelson.

Left: A gold miner in Eldorado Canyon. *Library of Congress.*

The former mining area of Nelson.

During the investigation, sounds of footsteps deeper in the tunnel system could be heard echoing. Sounds of rocks being tossed were heard nearby. Additionally, shadows were witnessed darting around the darkness of one tunnel, and murmurs of voices were heard.

Please note it is dangerous to investigate abandoned shafts without an experienced guide familiar with the location. Several mine shafts and cave systems in Nevada are not secure and have deep drops within them. Though some investigators for shows and documentaries are seen exploring these cave systems, it is not without any research or guidance from an expert in the area.

Looking back in time, Nelson and Eldorado Canyon were well established long before there was ever a thought of Las Vegas. Newcomers loved the remote, untamed region that was filled with many treasures.[26] The area was first discovered by the Spanish. Still, settlers from the East quickly moved into the region, taking control of the area, including the Techatticup Mine, founded in 1861. The remote location was attractive to prospectors, desperados and Civil War deserters looking for riches in a site where no one would find them. Having both Northern and Confederate

The abandoned mine shaft in Nelson where there are many reports of paranormal activity.

An old supply shed and gas pump in Nelson.

troops settling in the region, it was no wonder why tempers flared and what seemed to be a mini Civil War occurred in Eldorado as deserting soldiers from each side of the war continued to battle in their new sanctuary away from the main battlefront. As quickly as the town grew, it became known as an authentic western town with murderers and thieves, resulting in Nelson getting a rowdy reputation.

However, long before the Spanish settled the town in 1775, it was home to ancient Puebloan Indians. The Spaniards moved into the canyon searching for gold when they settled along the Colorado River, calling their settlement Eldorado.

During the time of lawlessness in Eldorado Canyon, the nearest sheriff was in Pioche, two hundred miles away. He did not even bother coming to town most of the time unless there was a murder. Even then, he did not always come to maintain peace in the village because it was so far out of the way.

Eventually, in 1941, the mine was fully depleted and closed, putting many prospectors and miners out of work. Many residents moved away, but Nelson eventually became a rest stop along Highway 165, with a gas station and a place for travelers to rest. However, the town was struck by flooding and eventually was abandoned. The miners left everything behind, including their dogs, upon leaving the town. Ultimately, the dogs died in the town, many within the abandoned cave systems. The sounds of these dogs can be heard howling through the caves, and they are known today as hellhounds.

However, it was later discovered that what was believed to be the first of many mining operations in Eldorado Canyon was not. Eldorado Canyon was first mined in 1851 by Santa Fe Trail explorer Francis X. Aubrey. He was traveling through the area and noticed bright yellowish and gold hues in the rocks, realizing gold was there. He made notes in his diary. Unfortunately, no one knew of his findings because he was killed on his way back to Santa Fe. It was not known he had discovered the gold until his diary was published in the 1960s.

CHAPTER 7
GOLD POINT

Gold Point is one of those secluded ghost towns that may take extra time to get to, but it is well worth the journey. This ghost town is one of the best preserved and takes visitors back in time to what life was like during the gold rush. Plus, it is the best place in Nevada to watch the stars. As quiet as Gold Point is today, it is near impossible to believe this small community was once a booming economy due to a significant silver and gold rush.

The town could have been forgotten like many other ghost towns in southern Nevada; however, thanks to the self-appointed town sheriff, Walter Kremin, this town has been slowly restored and preserved back to its condition when it was a booming community. As featured in *Real Haunts: Ghost Towns*, Sheriff Kremin, or Sheriff Stone, as many know him, stated, "They are there. I know they are there. They don't bother me none," regarding the spirits remaining in the town. Sheriff Kremin's experiences in the town confirmed the experiences many guests and paranormal investigators have had when visiting Gold Point.

Gold Point is hidden near the Nevada-California border in Esmeralda County, Nevada, southwest Goldfield. Back in the 1860s, this community was a thriving silver mining camp known as Lime Point. The small mining camp had 125 dwellings, a post office, a bakery, cafés, hotels, a general store and numerous saloons. Eventually, the community became known as Hornsilver until 1932, when it was renamed Gold Point.

The saloon in Gold Point is one of many remaining structures in the area.

Like many other ghost towns in southern Nevada, mining operations dwindled during World War II as the government ordered gold mines to shut down. The shutdowns were attempting to reallocate the mining workforce to help make weapons and other items for the war effort. As a result, Gold Point residents moved out of town, seeking other towns to continue earning money to support their way of life.

If it weren't for a Las Vegas wallpaper hanger, Herb Robbins, and his partner and now self-appointed sheriff of Gold Point, Walt Kremin, Gold Point as it is today may not exist.[27] In the 1970s, Herb and Chuck Kremin, Walt's brother, stumbled upon Gold Point and discovered an opportunity to purchase many of the deteriorating buildings. At the time, Gold Point was home to only a handful of residents, and many of the remaining structures needed some tender love and care.

Herb luckily hit the jackpot in Las Vegas, enabling the three to continue purchasing a majority of the town. The partnership purchased the post office, general store, many of the mining cabins and the home of Senator Harry Wiley. The home of Senator Wiley was complete with all the original furnishings, allowing the men to maintain a historical aspect of this once booming gold and silver mining town. With the help of many friends, areas of the town have been fully restored, and a sense of life back in the Old West has been resurrected.

Stepping into Gold Point is like stepping back in time. It is the place to go in southern Nevada to learn more about the Old West, mining operations and local history. When walking down the street, it feels like stepping into another world with old miners' cabins, the post office, a saloon, a hangman's noose and outhouses.

The location of Gold Point makes it the darkest spot in Nevada, which many love for the stargazing opportunities. However, not only the living enjoy this town. Several accounts of paranormal activity have been reported, and with all the darkness, this town is the perfect place for them to hide and live undisturbed. Some guests who have stayed in the miners' cabins report hearing footsteps when lying in bed and hearing a knock on the door only to have no one there when opening it. Some have even reported seeing shadow figures in their cabins, walking down the street and in the saloon. On rare occasions, some guests have reported seeing ghostly apparitions in the corner of their cabin, watching and observing them.

Ora Mae Wiley was Gold Point's postmistress from 1940 to 1964. She passed away in 1980 at the age of eighty-three, and it is rumored that her spirit still lingers within the town. Some say she remains in Gold Point, continuing her daily duties as postmistress. Some believe she is the figure seen walking down the street and knocking on the cabin doors as she drops off mail to the miners.

While walking through the town, sounds of music and playful chatter could be heard from inside one of the bars in Gold Point. During a visit to the town, a paranormal research group experienced hearing these sounds

CHAPTER 8

GOLDFIELD

G oldfield, also known as the "Last Great Gold Camp," is the one town most everyone thinks about when discussing ghost towns and paranormal activity. It's one of the busiest living ghost towns in southern Nevada, with several residents living in the community, unique facts and chilling ghost stories. Though some residents still live in Goldfield, the population today, compared to back when it was booming, is drastically different; it is easy to see why it is classified as a ghost town. Even walking down the streets, it feels like no one else is in the area and makes one wonder if people still live in the community.

This chapter will contain historical information about the town and its former residents. It will also cover some of the most famously haunted locations, such as the Goldfield Hotel, the courthouse, the Goldfield Cemetery and the International Car Forest of the Last Church. There will also be information and an inside look into the eerie stories from within the Florence Mine from the first paranormal team to investigate the property.

Chances are, anyone who has visited Goldfield has a story of a ghostly encounter to share. Whether it was from their own experience or a story a resident shared with them in passing, many spooky stories about this ghost town are shared every day.

As a boomtown back in the day, Goldfield's population started to rise in 1902, when gold was discovered in the region. At its peak, the town had more than 20,000 residents and was the largest city in Nevada. During the town's early days, millions of dollars' worth of gold was discovered. However, the

The city of Goldfield as seen from the Florence Mine.

town's success was brought to a halt in 1923, when a fire destroyed most of the town. Luckily, many of the town's larger structures, including the haunted Goldfield Hotel, were saved, while many of the smaller businesses and homes fell victim to the roaring flames of this fire. Today, approximately 250 residents live and work in Goldfield.[29]

Goldfield was known as the Last Great Gold Camp and was definitely the place prospectors, entrepreneurs and those looking for a better life desired to live and work. Almost every day, it felt as if someone new was making their way to Goldfield searching for their American dream. The town was so enticing that many big names in the Wild West flocked to the region, including Virgil and Wyatt Earp, who called it home in the early 1900s. In fact, Virgil was the town's sheriff in 1904.

In the years leading up to 1905, Goldfield was transforming into a proper town. Sounds of construction filled the air day and night as contractors worked around the clock to meet the demand of buildings and homes that needed to be built. It seemed as if every day, a new building constructed of brick and stone filled the town's streets. Plus, the arrival of the Goldfield Railroad in September of the same year increased the desire to live in the community.

By 1906, Goldfield was making headlines across the country. On January 6, 1906, the *Sea Coast Echo* of Bay St. Louis, Missouri, published that Goldfield had "250 incorporated mining companies and instead of the barren desert of four years ago, is a hustling, bustling up-to-date city of 8,000 inhabitants."[30] Residents and local politicians had high hopes for

Goldfield, as the Esmeralda County seat was moved from Hawthorne to Goldfield in 1907.[31]

With the increase in mining operations throughout the area and the harsh working conditions, it was no surprise that in 1906, Goldfield mine owners were hit with many labor disputes. The Industrial Workers of the World and the Western Federation of Miners tried to control labor in the district, resulting in fierce labor disputes, which required federal troops to be sent to the area in December 1907 to restore peace and order to the community.

As with any town in the West, Goldfield experienced highs and lows, following a typical ebb and flow of success and disaster. In the 1910s, ore production experienced a steep decline, almost coming to a complete halt. However, the ore decline was just the beginning of the end for Goldfield. Those who were not finding any gold, silver or other rare minerals in the area packed up and either moved west to California, headed to another mining town or returned east. As townspeople headed out of town, the population of Goldfield took a drop to approximately five thousand residents staying behind.

Several years after the labor disputes were resolved, Goldfield experienced the first of many devastating events. In 1913, a significant flood submerged the town, sweeping away many buildings. According to the *Eureka Sentinel*, on September 13, 1913, "Goldfield was swept by the torrent from a cloudburst Saturday, and two women lost their lives."[32]

The few residents were helping support the town, but in 1923, a catastrophic fire ravaged the Main Street area in the city, burning many of the buildings within twenty-five blocks to the ground. After this fire, Goldfield was never the same and was never looked on as the exciting and significant community it once was.

According to the Associated Press and reported by the *Perth Amboy Evening News* on July 7, 1923, Goldfield was "swept by fire."[33] The desert breeze helped the blaze, which was believed by Fire Chief I.N. Galliac to have been set by a bootleggers' feud, engulf this once booming town. The article reported that the flames swept from end to end of the community. The fire killed one person (John Duryer, a janitor at the National Hotel) and caused another man to have a heart attack as he watched his shoe business burn to the ground (David D. McArthur). A woman was reported missing, and the fire caused an estimated $1.5 million in damages.

Goldfield had little time to recover from the fires in 1923, as another devastating fire swept through the community on September 29, 1924. The

A view looking into an abandoned building in Goldfield.

Goldfield News Building and the Montezuma Club fell victim to this fire. After this, Goldfield slowly became a ghostly image of its former, lively self.

At its peak, Goldfield was a proper modern city of its time. The community was served by three railroads, five newspapers, two mining stock exchanges, five banks, dozens of saloons and four schools. Some of these historic buildings remain, and those surviving the fires and floods are some of the most haunted locations found in southern Nevada. Learning all the death, destruction and misfortunate luck residents endured while living in Goldfield almost makes one wonder if the area was cursed.

GOLDFIELD HOTEL

One of the most famous buildings in Goldfield is the Goldfield Hotel, which still stands today. When construction started in 1907, this enormous brick building cost around $400,000 to build. Although it is no longer open for business, the hotel is in the center of town, watching over the area, offering the ideal location for Goldfield's spirits to hang out and watch the townspeople and tourists walk through the Main Street area.

Many paranormal researchers wonder who or what remains within the emptiness of the Goldfield Hotel. Theories claim everything from a lady of the night to a demon and George Wingfield himself to small children haunts the hotel. Though many have their theories, the most shared story is that of Elizabeth, who haunts room 109 of the hotel.[34] Elizabeth was a pregnant prostitute who was believed to have been carrying Wingfield's baby. As the hotel's owner and a significant figure within the community, he wanted to maintain his reputation and trapped her in the room. To keep her from sharing the news, he chained her to the radiator in room 109. One story claims she gave birth in the room she was being held captive in, and then at night, Wingfield threw the newborn to its death down an old mining shaft the hotel sits over, leaving Elizabeth alone in her room to die.

Several investigators have claimed to have encountered what they believe to be the spirit of Elizabeth hanging around room 109. Some have seen her looking sadly out the windows of the same room. In addition, disembodied voices have been heard throughout the hotel. Disembodied voices include EVP captures of a baby crying in the basement and the sobbing cries of a woman on the second floor. Others have claimed to feel Elizabeth's presence and have felt psychic impressions of her overwhelming sadness.

With the reports of Elizabeth haunting the Goldfield Hotel, could it be possible Wingfield remains behind? There are many locations throughout Goldfield where Wingfield has been spotted, and several people have reported seeing his apparition walking through the halls of his hotel. Some accounts claim he leaves behind ashes from the cigars he smokes in the afterlife. Some

The Goldfield Hotel sits abandoned on a cold, snowy February morning.

believe he remains at the hotel out of guilt for how he treated Elizabeth and the other sins he committed while alive and living in Goldfield.

What seems the oddest about the story of room 109 is that when the baby was born, it was supposedly tossed down the hotel's mine shaft. However, there was no mine shaft in or around the hotel until 1925. The mine shaft was created long after Wingfield sold the hotel. Additionally, there are no accounts of a prostitute named Elizabeth in Goldfield. So could this story be an urban legend? Is it based on fact? Or a combination of both? Either way, many have experienced paranormal activity around room 109 and in the hotel's basement, where the mine shaft was reported to have been located.

When the Goldfield Hotel was thriving, it was the place for visitors, especially high-profile guests and many families. The place was lively and the place to be for all the action in town. Imagining what the hotel was like in its heyday, it is easy to envision children running around, playing on the elaborate staircase. At the same time, parents sat around socializing, and couples dressed in their finest attire strolled through the lobby. It appears that some of the excitement from when the hotel was in operation remains behind today. Several paranormal investigators have reported seeing the ghosts of small children laughing and playing on the lobby's staircase. Also, let's not forget the spirits of former hotel visitors who continue to pass through, only staying at the hotel for short periods each time they manifest at the hotel.

One of the creepiest guests rumored to have stayed at the Goldfield Hotel in the afterlife is "the Stabber." Locals claim he lurks in a particular area of the main dining room—the Gold Room—with a kitchen knife. Though no one has been injured by the blade he wields, he does cause a fright in all those who see him. Typically, this spirit disappears seconds after lunging out at people who enter the room.

In addition to the spirits of former guests, the halls are full of shadow people who have been spotted. Sounds of boots walking around and a man's voice mumbling to himself have been captured on audio equipment. Scents of cigar smoke, flowers, perfumes and colognes have filled the hotel's air. One gets an odd feeling standing in front of the hotel, and it definitely feels like something is watching from within. It is no wonder why the Goldfield Hotel is considered one of the most haunted locations in the world.

The Goldfield Hotel is a favorite location for paranormal researchers to investigate and explore. Many investigators, such as Brian J. Rollins, co-founder of SisBro Paranormal in Las Vegas, Nevada, have investigated the hotel multiple times. He said he and his sister, Elizabeth, have investigated the Goldfield Hotel at least a half-dozen times. Though they have investigated the hotel many times, he claims their most recent investigation was the most interesting.

Rollins was joined with about five other investigators and experienced a peaceful pre-investigation walkthrough of the building. After the walkthrough, the group split up and went to different areas of the hotel, and the investigation began. Here is his story about investigating the Goldfield Hotel:

"My sister Elizabeth and I went to the second floor, and we immediately started having equipment malfunctions and experiencing strange sensations and off feelings. We decided to go to the third floor and meet up with everyone else. We all started feeling the same odd sense, and it felt like someone, or something, did not want us there.

"We started to head downstairs," Rollins recalls. "Then suddenly we heard the sounds of boots chasing after us. Additionally, we suddenly started getting stomachaches."

Later in the investigation, Rollins shared that one of the female investigators who was hosting the investigation event at the Goldfield Hotel was pushed by an unseen force into another investigator. This experience was witnessed by others in the group.

Even though Rollins and the rest of the group he was with were having strange experiences, it didn't stop them from continuing their investigation of the hotel. He continued to share his story:

"After a short discussion, we decided to investigate the hotel lobby and then visit Elizabeth's room. However, it felt like whoever or whatever did not want us in the hotel was still following us around and making things extremely uncomfortable. Finally, things were getting too uncomfortable for us, resulting in our decision to put all of our equipment away and get ready to leave the hotel.

"As we were packing things up, the odd feelings started to subside. Since one of the investigators with us had not been in the basement, and since we all were feeling better, we decided to go downstairs.

"Soon after arriving in the basement," Rollins continued, "the entity making us uncomfortable found our group again. It felt like it was herding us out. I mentioned to everyone we needed to leave immediately, and we did."

After leaving the hotel, Rollins and his sister felt like they were still being affected as they drove twenty-six miles to their hotel. He claims he has never encountered such a strong presence, and for it to affect six people, all in the same way for such a long time, he added, "I can only say, 'Wow!'"

Goldfield Cemetery

The Goldfield Cemetery, also known as "the Last Dig," was initially located in the center of town. However, when the railroad depot was built, the train dropped passengers off at the entrance to the final resting place for many townspeople. The cemetery near the train depot was not the best way to welcome newcomers to a town as brilliant as Goldfield. With the decision made to relocate the cemetery to another part of town, the group of men put in charge of the move dubbed themselves the Official Ghouls of the Night. These men conducted a clandestine exhumation of every body buried in the cemetery, carefully relocating them and their headstones to their present-day resting places in a single night in 1908.

The cemetery as it sits today is full of crudely crafted headstones and some more delicate-looking gravestones identifying the occupants below. Several visitors have reported encounters with ghostly figures; many are believed to be victims of local mining accidents, gunshot wounds and even a lonely fellow who died from eating library paste.

The Goldfield Cemetery is an interesting place to explore and learn more about the town's former residents.

More than 1,200 people are buried in the Goldfield Cemetery. The creepiest thing about walking through the Goldfield Cemetery is that the number of dead in the cemetery outweighs the residents in town. Strolling through the cemetery reveals the lives of many who came from around the world and spent their final days in Goldfield. People from all corners of the earth made their way to Goldfield for freedom, wealth and to start a new life. Tombstones reveal names of all ethnicities, showing how diverse a community Goldfield truly was.

It was known that many who served in the Civil War made their way west after General Robert E. Lee surrendered at Appomattox Courthouse in Virginia. For example, Civil War veteran Joseph Brown, first lieutenant of the Seventy-Eighth Regiment of Pennsylvania, died in 1906 and is buried in the cemetery. Confederate soldier W.A. Marmaduke was also buried in the graveyard after settling in Goldfield after the war. Upon visiting, Marmaduke's grave was full of bottle caps, whiskey bottles, coins and other remnants of those who visited to pay their respects.

During an EVP session at Marmaduke's grave, all things were quiet until a woman's faint voice was heard during an attempt to reach Marmaduke

The Goldfield Cemetery is the final resting place for many residents and is reportedly one of the most haunted areas in the town.

himself. So why did the paranormal team hear a female voice and not get a response from Marmaduke? The most likely explanation is that cemeteries are not as haunted as many would like to believe. Sure, they are creepy, but spirits tend to hang out in areas where they are comfortable and enjoy spending time. So chances are unless they visited a loved one in the cemetery, it is rare to encounter a spirit with their grave.

This theory does not mean that cemeteries are not haunted. The female voice captured could have been the spirit of a woman who frequented the cemetery visiting a loved one. Plus, because so many want to believe a cemetery is a place to go for paranormal activity, many inexperienced paranormal investigators head to cemeteries to conjure up something they are not prepared to deal with. Those are the spirits and entities many encounter when visiting a cemetery.

On the other hand, one theory about paranormal activity is that sometimes the spirits do not know they are dead and continue with their daily routine. This theory is why so many head to the cemetery in hopes of communicating with John F. Meagher. Meagher was found dead in a grave he was digging in the Goldfield Cemetery. He was seventy-three years of age, and he died in 1918 when blasting a boulder to dig a grave in the Catholic section of the cemetery. A piece of the rock entered his brain during the blast, and he was laid to rest in the very grave he was attempting to dig. Recent attempts to reach Meagher have been unsuccessful, which means chances are he has moved on or found another place to spend his afterlife haunting.

It is rumored several shadow people dart around the cemetery and lurk behind tombstones and trees. Others have reported ghost lights, disembodied voices and feelings of being watched when paying their respects to those buried in the Goldfield Cemetery.

THE GOLDFIELD EMPORIUM

The Goldfield Emporium is a store set in the Main Street area of Goldfield across the street from the Goldfield Hotel. This store offers various unique items, including antiques, bottles, jewelry, books and more. The back area behind the store is a train museum with a replica of Goldfield and the immediate surrounding area.

The store, especially the building's basement, is rumored to be haunted. Those working the store and paranormal investigators have heard strange noises coming from the basement, footsteps and disembodied voices. Several have seen shadow people roaming the store and train display room. Some paranormal investigators have claimed to feel a negative presence following them when in the basement of the building. They claim it is very frightening and unwelcoming. Some have claimed to want to get out of the area as fast as possible.

GOLDFIELD HIGH SCHOOL

Another famously haunted building in Goldfield is the Goldfield High School, which is said to have several entities, including a young female student wandering the halls.

The Goldfield High School was built in 1907 and was a state-of-the-art educational facility. The three-story building, with a basement, was one of the few remaining buildings in town to beat the odds of surviving the many Goldfield disasters. The school was the most prominent and best-equipped

An abandoned school in Goldfield. *Library of Congress.*

high school at the time in Nevada. The building was the community's pride and joy, mainly because it was home to the only standard-sized basketball court in the state other than the one located at the University of Nevada. The Goldfield High School graduated its last class in 1952.

Today, the Goldfield High School sits abandoned but still houses its original desks, chairs and chalkboards. Some of the walls still have writing on them from former students. Even looking at this building from the outside is enough to put shivers down a person's spine as they take in the complete abandonment of the structure. Inside, the floors, baseboards, lighting and furniture are covered in layers of dust from many decades of being left alone. Door frames and corners of rooms are adorned with cobwebs, which contribute to the creepiness of the Goldfield High School.

Rumors surrounding paranormal activity include that of the one schoolgirl who still roams the halls today. Others have reported seeing the apparitions of two schoolgirls and a small boy. During an investigation, the small boy has been known to play around with a beach ball brought by paranormal researchers. During one investigation, sounds of high heels walking up the stairs were heard. The sounds continued to grow louder, passed by the investigator and continued walking down the hallway.

Several people have reported seeing dark shadows and light anomalies, hearing disembodied voices and unexplained sounds and feeling cold spots throughout the building. During an interview, one paranormal investigator, Williamson, stated that during his first investigation of the high school in 2015, he and the other investigators he was with heard what sounded like a girl's loud scream coming from the shower room. Upon further investigation, no one was in the shower room. During the same investigation, he also heard footsteps going down a flight of stairs and sounds of kids running up and down the second-floor hallway and had an uncomfortable feeling he was being followed everywhere he went in the high school.

The Goldfield High School is another popular location for paranormal researchers to investigate. Paranormal investigator Rollins enjoys investigating the high school as much as he enjoys investigating the Goldfield Hotel and has several stories to share about his paranormal experiences at the location.

According to Rollins, one night when they were investigating the English Room, the group started talking about a name written on the chalkboard. Rollins then started sharing a story about how Willy, a student of the Goldfield High School in the early 1900s, had stolen a lipstick and written his name on the chalkboard. After sharing the story with the group, he captured an EVP that claimed, "It wasn't me!"

During another trip to the Goldfield High School, Rollins and his sister, Elizabeth, split up to investigate different building areas. His sister went into the girls' bathroom in the basement, and he went to the Science Room. He was not getting too much activity and was about to wrap up his investigation. Being the respectful investigator he is, Rollins said, "Thank you," as he left the Science Room and invited any spirits in the area to follow him to other areas of the school.

While collecting his equipment, he heard a male voice say, "Hello, Betsy." Immediately, Rollins asked, "What did you say?" This interaction was captured as an EVP on his digital voice recorder. A few seconds later, he heard footsteps coming up the stairs, followed by his sister walking into the room. Rollins thought this was an intriguing experience because they called his sister Betsy.

They did a follow-up with the people who ran the investigations in the high school and played the EVP back for them. They checked to see if any students who attended the Goldfield High School were called Betsy, but they could not find any.

According to the paranormal stories circulating, it seems as if the Science Room in the Goldfield High School is one of the most active rooms in the building. It is also one room where Rollins appears to have had many experiences. He recalled during one of his very first high school investigations, it felt like they were not getting anything. The room was quiet and still. Rollins and his sister decided to leave the room and find another area of the high school to conduct an EVP session. Upon leaving the room, his sister said something about the students not being in the room that night. When the two returned home and reviewed their evidence, they discovered they were not alone in the Science Room. They had captured an EVP that said "…but we are…" in response to Elizabeth stating there were no students in the room.

Could the Goldfield High School be haunted by former students, teachers or staff? There is a strong possibility, especially since everyone loved the building and was enamored by its architecture and state-of-the-art features.

Esmeralda County Courthouse

The Esmeralda County Courthouse is a building still actively being used today. The courthouse has always been used for that purpose since it was built in 1907 and is currently protected under the greater Goldfield Historic District. This building is an amazing location, providing a look into Goldfield's historical past while at the same time allowing residents to pay for speeding tickets, get a marriage license and renew their driver's license.

The two-story courthouse resembles a castle and is another building in the community with reports of paranormal activity. Why wouldn't spirits want to hang out at the courthouse? This building has been very well preserved, with original flooring, lamps and other furnishings found throughout. One of the most interesting paranormal accounts in the Esmeralda County Courthouse is that of a phantom trial, complete with voices being heard in the courtroom. Other paranormal encounters include shadow people walking the halls and a ghostly hangman's noose spotted in one of the chambers.

Staff at the courthouse have reported experiencing a haunted chair that moves independently. One night before going home, the staff had locked the chair in a vault on the first floor. The following day when they returned, the chair was next to its desk, which meant it went through the steel door of the vault—which was still locked—and into another room on its own. The doors had been locked, and no one else had entered the courthouse until the staff returned the following day.

Nixon Building and Cook Building

Down the road from the Goldfield Hotel are two buildings with a tragic past of their own and plenty of paranormal stories. The Nixon Building and the Cook Building may not have famous stories like the hotel and high school, but these two buildings have some ghostly rumors going around town.

The Nixon Building was owned by George Nixon and Wingfield, who in 1906 organized the Goldfield Consolidated Mines. In 1909, Nixon took the bank building, and Wingfield took the mines when the company was dissolved. The Cook Building, also referred to as the Bank Building, has had many lives, including being a paranormal museum, bank, hotel, offices and café. John S. Cook opened the bank doors in January 1905 in a small shack before moving to its current location.[35]

Some have claimed to see the spirit of Claudie, an employee who died after being thrown down the stairwell from the third floor of the Cook Building. To this day, her assailant is unknown, but some believe it could have been Cook, whom she threatened to out for an affair and possibly some unethical banking practices. Other reports include hearing footsteps in the stairwells, hearing disembodied voices in both buildings and seeing ghostly figures peering out of windows at onlookers down below.

Santa Fe Motel and Saloon

The Santa Fe Motel and Saloon, formerly the Santa Fe Club, is where prospectors and mine workers headed when it was quitting time. Being located on the outskirts of town, this building was saved from the flood and fires that ravaged the town. Today, it is possible to enjoy a beverage with locals and some miners from Goldfield's past who still stop by for a drink at quitting time.

As the longest-operating business in Goldfield, it is still possible to pull up a barstool, shoot the bull with locals and reminisce about what life was like more than one hundred years ago, back when the saloon opened in 1905. Heck, it might even be possible to get firsthand accounts of what happened from the patrons who have been returning to the saloon since its opening.

Paranormal claims at the Santa Fe Motel and Saloon include light anomalies, disembodied voices, sounds of a gathering, shadow people and the sensation of being watched.

The Earp Brothers

Two of Goldfield's most famous residents were the Earp brothers.[36] The two brothers had always been attracted to boomtowns, and the promise Goldfield once offered newcomers was very intriguing to Virgil and Wyatt. In July 1904, after selling all of their belongings, Virgil and his wife, Allie, arrived in Goldfield. When the couple was on their last dollar, Virgil was hired as a special officer to watch over the high-stakes gambling tables at the National Club. In January 1905, he was sworn in as deputy sheriff by the Esmeralda County sheriff.

Soon after, his brother Wyatt came to visit for a few days in February of the same year, and it is believed that he worked at Tex Rickard's Northern Saloon. It is unclear how long Wyatt stayed in Goldfield or how often he returned to see his brother, but several reports claim he did spend a significant amount of time there visiting before Virgil's death later that year.

After recovering from pneumonia in February 1905, Virgil had a relapse at the start of October. On October 19, 1905, he died from illness with Allie by his side at St. Mary's Hospital in Goldfield. Per his request, his remains were buried in Riverview Cemetery in Portland, Oregon.

So the biggest question remains: do the Earp brothers haunt Goldfield? Some would say yes because that is where Virgil spent his remaining days. At the same time, others would say no because that is not where the two spent a significant part of their lives. However, some visitors and residents have claimed to have seen a man resembling photos of Virgil Earp with his long, beautifully full mustache walking down the Main Street area of Goldfield. So one or both of the brothers might be still lingering in Goldfield today.

Florence Mine

The Florence Mine still stands overlooking the town of Goldfield. Though it is no longer a working mine, the property has been well maintained and restored by the current owner, Jon Aurich. Upon passing through the mine's property gates, many emotions fill the air—happiness, sadness, desperation and desire. Like the town of Goldfield, the Florence Mine had its share of ups and downs throughout the years.

The Florence Mine had several owners and many prospectors who leased and worked the land throughout the years. Finally, in 1902, Charlie Taylor

The Florence Mine is no longer operating but has been beautifully restored by Jon Aurich.

located the Florence Mine and several other mining claims in the area.[37] In 1904, the mine was leased by a man named Sweeney, and that was the start of ownership changing like the mine had a revolving door. Soon after, Tom Lockhart, with partner A.D. Parker, bought half interest in the Florence Mine. Eventually, the two took control of it.

When Wingfield and Nixon organized the Goldfield Consolidated Mines in 1906, they set their sights on purchasing the Florence Mine. Lockhart did not want to sell any part of his interest in the mine; however, the mine did sell shares to help pay for equipment and operations. An article in the *Lovelock Tribune* on December 21, 1906, shared information about Wingfield and Nixon purchasing shares in the Florence Mine.[38]

In 1908, the Florence Mine was the site of the last major mill in Goldfield and had forty stamps and processed approximately 160 tons a day. Unfortunately, the mill was struck by a fire on December 11, 1911, destroying it and other structures on the property.[39] Luckily, according to Aurich, the service buildings on the property were spared from the fire.

In 1916, the Florence Mine went into receivership after Lockhart retired and moved to California. From 1916 through 1922, several different mining

Entrance to the mine shaft at the Florence Mine in Goldfield.

companies took control of the Florence Mine. Unfortunately, many did not stay long when they discovered the mine was not producing the significant return they had hoped for. Then Martin Duffy came to Goldfield intending to be a successful miner. In 1923, at the age of twenty-three, Duffy leased the Florence Mine and discovered a pillar in the mine, which was a success for him. The mine produced $160,000 in gold within the first six months. In 1944, Duffy married Ruth Grove, a local schoolteacher.

Martin and Ruth worked the mine together, and in 1952, they were able to purchase half ownership of the mine. They established a residence by moving a small house onto the property. He worked the mine until 1971, when he was killed in a mining accident.

In 1982, Jon Aurich traveled to Goldfield because of his interest in mining towns after being introduced to them by his father. During his visit, Aurich met Ruth Duffy, who took a liking to him. The two shared interest in Goldfield's history and mining operations. Unfortunately, Ruth passed away in 1995, leaving her holdings of the Florence Mine to Jon. Since then, he has maintained the mine, making it a true historical treasure.

Today, the mine remains home to the spirits that once worked, lived and explored the land. One paranormal research team visited the Florence Mine to do some filming and be the first team to investigate the property. Needless to say, their investigation revealed far more than they could ever have imagined.

Side note: The following details contain information gathered firsthand by the author, who was part of the paranormal research team invited to investigate the Florence Mine in February 2020.

AFTER DRIVING UP THE driveway, there was a small shack to the right of the owner's residence. Shadows of a man watching through the window were spotted, and throughout the two-day investigation, the same shadow appeared, as if he was watching to make sure the team treated the property with respect.

The Florence Mine is the only location in the Goldfield Historic Mining District to have a still standing, preserved Hoist House. The investigation

The Florence Mine is a well-preserved piece of history in Goldfield.

started in the Hoist House, which is fully intact with all original machinery and tools. Set on the operator's chair were a newspaper and a pair of eyeglasses dating back to when the mine was in full operation. This building was like stepping back in time and offered many opportunities to experience time with the former workers of the mine. In addition, Aurich shared some paranormal accounts about the building, including the feeling of not being alone, hearing voices and seeing light anomalies in the storage room of the Hoist House.

During an EVP session in the storage room, a darker-than-dark shadow person stood in the corner observing, but the rest of the session was uneventful. The author heard men's voices chatting in the main room of the Hoist House, and she went to investigate. No one was in the other room, and she checked outside to make sure no one was out there talking. The area was clear. She continued hearing the voices, which sounded like men talking about their work and what needed to be done before the end of the day. Then, as suddenly as the voices started, they ended.

Later that night, the paranormal researchers were invited to spend the night in the mine owner's residence. It was a fascinating evening. While the

Inside the Hoist House at the Florence Mine, where many artifacts from the past remain.

team, Aurich and his family were chatting in the living room, there was an odd scent of something burning. A wood-burning fireplace heated the room, but that was not the smell. Upon further investigation, nothing was burning, and the scent resembled what it smelled like when a headlamp was burning. Aurich demonstrated how the headlamps worked, and then suddenly, the burning smell disappeared.

Before going to bed, one of the investigators spotted what appeared to be a woman walking around the room. He described the woman to the owner, who then walked over to the dining room wall and pulled a picture from it. Upon showing the photo to the investigator, the spirit in the home was quickly identified as Ruth Duffy, one of the mine's former owners, who passed the property on to Aurich.

Also present in the home were glimpses of a male spirit who greatly resembled the photos of Tom Lockart. It is very possible he was the same spirit that was seen watching over everyone as they slept in the living room. The two researchers spending the night in the home were woken up throughout the night by seeing the shadows of a male spirit walking around the room, in the hallway outside the living room area and in the living room. The creaking from his steps could be heard, but other than that, he remained silent as he walked around the home.

In the middle of the night, the author was woken by someone yelling into her ear, "I didn't start the fire!" Startled, she jumped up on the couch she was sleeping on to realize no one else was awake in the room. So who was this entity that yelled so desperately into her ear? It is still unknown, but could it have been someone accused of starting the fires at the mine? Or could it have been someone charged with creating the fires in the town? Who the voice belonged to remains a mystery, but it was indeed a unique experience that got her heart beating fast.

During the second day of the investigation, the team investigated a collapsed mine shaft. As the team entered through a small hole in the ground supported by decaying wood beams, they knew they were not alone. The farther they descended into the mine, the smaller the area they could walk in grew. There were some parts of the shaft where the team almost had to crawl to continue moving forward. Once the mine shaft entrance was out of sight, there was a small area where the team could stand up. The site was so small that only the three members could fit comfortably without bumping into one another.

The investigation of this area was very quiet. Nothing paranormal occurred or was captured during the photo, video or EVP sessions. A spirit

Above: Entrance to a collapsed mine shaft at the Florence Mine in Goldfield.

Opposite, top: A closer look into the mine shaft at the Florence Mine in Goldfield.

Opposite, bottom: A noose is discovered inside the Mill House at the Florence Mine in Goldfield.

box session also revealed nothing. However, the author noticed another shaft continuing just past where the team was standing. She decided to crawl back to see where it led to. Not too far back, it ended in a pile of rubble from when the mine had collapsed. It is unconfirmed if there were any men trapped in the mine when it collapsed, but it is rumored several men died in this area of the mine.

Once up against the rubble from the collapse, she started to get dizzy and had trouble breathing. In reality, what was only a few minutes felt like hours to her. Quickly, she was overwhelmed with emotions, crying herself, struggling to breathe and feeling like she was being crushed. Then she heard voices crying out as she continued struggling to breathe. Not being able to take the emotions and the pressure she was feeling, the author left the collapsed area of the mine, heading back to where the rest of her team was. Once she was back with the others, she felt perfectly fine—almost as if nothing had happened.

In the next part of the investigation, the team separated, and one investigator went down into the main mine shaft with Aurich's son. While down there, he heard many things and knew he was not alone. The two were down there for more than thirty minutes, and when he emerged from the shaft, he was not himself. The other investigators could see he was a little off-balance, short of breath and dizzy. Whatever was down in the mine with him psychically attacked him.

While the investigation of the mine shaft was underway, the author took time to talk with Aurich's daughter to learn more about her experiences at the Florence Mine. Speaking with the daughter revealed that she was sometimes afraid to go to different areas of the mine. For example, standing outside the Mill House, the daughter claimed she could see men looking out of the windows at her. She shared that some of the male spirits would talk to her, telling her they wanted to harm her. She said they would speak to her in an attempt to lure her into the Mill House, which she was always afraid to go into alone. One of the male spirits even told her to walk

A look at the Mill House at the Florence Mine, where apparitions of men have been spotted.

underneath a very unstable swinging beam that was hanging from one of the structures between the Mill House and the Hoist House.

Upon further investigation, two team members went into the Mill House. They felt like they were being followed and could hear footsteps walking behind them. Up in the rafters, it appeared as if there were a few shadow people following them as they explored the building. While looking up at the shadows, the author discovered a noose hanging from the rafters. Upon speaking with the mine's owner, it was learned that the noose was not there the other day when they were in the building. Was this noose a manifestation of something that had happened in the past? Or was it something someone placed in the building when no one was at the mine? There are many possibilities, but it seemed as if the spirits were leading the investigators to this area of the building to discover the noose. It felt as if the spirits were trying to tell the investigators something.

One more strange occurrence experienced at the Florence Mine: strange knocking sounds heard randomly. They were heard when exploring the Mill House and around various mine shafts and entrances. Were these sounds those of Tommy-Knockers, or were they just normal sounds coming from within the mine and old buildings? The question remains unanswered, which is what the Tommy-Knockers like. These mischievous creatures continue to stay in the shadows of southern Nevada ghost towns, going about their business as they always have.

The research team's experience at the Florence Mine is truly one they will never forget.

THE INTERNATIONAL CAR FOREST OF THE LAST CHURCH

It was created in 2002 by longtime Goldfield resident Michael Mark Rippie, who dropped a car off onto the eighty-acre property to act as a new canvas style for artists. From there, he added forty more cars from his junkyard to serve as a blank slate for artists looking to expand their creativity. He was joined by Chad Sorg, who was driving through town on his way back to Reno. He stopped to talk with Rippie, and together they made the International Car Forest of the Last Church what it is today. The site is the largest of its kind in the country, even surpassing Carhenge in Nebraska.

The International Car Forest of the Last Church is a unique roadside attraction in Goldfield.

The International Car Forest of the Last Church is home to more than forty vehicles, including a mix of cars, trucks, vans and buses. All have been delicately balanced on their front or back ends, and some have been stacked on top of one another. All vehicles have been uniquely painted, including everything from ghosts to skulls and caricatures of politicians to aliens.

The site was officially named with "the Last Church" in the title for Rippie's personal beliefs that reject organized religion.

Following an angry falling out, Rippie and Sorg no longer work together, but the site remains a roadside attraction in Goldfield. Unfortunately, it is set back off the road, and those not paying attention may miss out on this exciting display of graffiti art.

One intriguing item at the International Car Forest of the Last Church is the small grave set far back up against the hill. Not much was written on the headstone, outside of the name Jessie S. Linebarger and the date 1916–?? (unreadable death year). The grave was small and had a train in the headstone.

A lonely grave sits alone at the International Car Forest of the Last Church in Goldfield.
Sharon Artlip.

According to Sharon Artlip, president of the International Car Forest of the Last Church, the headstone has been on the property for years and always treated with respect. She said the individual named on the headstone was involved in the railroads and lived and worked in the Goldfield area. To help preserve the site, Artlip said they have plans to put a small picket fence around it to keep people from driving over the grave.

As far as paranormal activity at the International Car Forest of the Last Church, Artlip said there had been many paranormal investigators at the site, especially around the headstone. However, she typically does not go out to the site at night, and no one has shared any specific paranormal activity with her. Additionally, there are no reports of paranormal activity, but being set in Goldfield, chances are there are a few spirits who linger there. Remember, anything is possible when it comes to the paranormal in this ghost town.

To fully experience the spirits in Goldfield, it is best to not complain about the twenty-five-mile-per-hour speed limit through town but to put the car in park and go exploring. Take time to walk in front of the Goldfield Hotel, where you can feel the tension resonate from within the brick walls. Go shopping at the Goldfield Emporium, where you might encounter a ghost or two shopping with you. Take a moment to sit down and speak with the spirits lingering at the Goldfield Cemetery and see if you can encounter Mr. Meagher yourself. With so many paranormal activity reports, it is nearly impossible to throw a stone and not have it fly through a spirit. You will not be alone when walking the streets of Goldfield, which means your ghostly tour guides will provide you with a one-of-a-kind experience like no other ghost town in southern Nevada.

CHAPTER 9
GOODSPRINGS AND PRIMM

Just outside the Las Vegas area sits the ghost town of Goodsprings. Those who visit Goodsprings love being able to experience and enjoy an authentic Wild West ghost town adventure. Exploring this ghost town provides many opportunities to roll back the pages of history and encounter some genuinely fascinating spirits.

Like many other ghost towns in southern Nevada, Goodsprings was a very successful and bountiful mining district. As a result, many flocked to the area in hopes of achieving their goals of becoming the next successful prospector in the West. Unfortunately, as with all the other ghost towns, this community boomed quickly before suddenly losing its momentum, forcing many residents to abandon their homes, hopes and dreams.

Early mining claims in Goodsprings started as early as 1868 but remained in the shadows of all the other mining discoveries in southern Nevada. It was not until 1902 that the Keystone Mine was discovered, and the Yellow Pine Mining Company acquired it. Within the first couple of years, the mine produced eighty-five million pounds of zinc and lead. This discovery put Goodsprings on the map, and tents and cabins started popping up, making it a proper boomtown.

Joseph Good ran cattle in the Spring Mountains and Goodsprings areas, and the town was eventually named after him. The first signs of buildings began to emerge in the community between 1910 and 1911. The town was home to a post office, several saloons, the *Weekly Gazette*, a general store and the Goodsprings Schoolhouse.

By World War I, the town had a population of approximately eight hundred people. This was definitely not the same type of boom as larger towns such as Goldfield and Rhyolite experienced, but Goodsprings continued to boom and be successful through World War II. Shortly after the war ended, the town's population began to dwindle slowly. Today, approximately two hundred people live in Goodsprings, helping preserve historic buildings, including the Goodsprings Schoolhouse and the Pioneer Saloon.

Pioneer Saloon

Goodsprings is home to one of the oldest watering holes in southern Nevada: the Pioneer Saloon, which opened in 1913. It is difficult to visit this saloon without having a paranormal encounter. Many have left the Pioneer Saloon with stories about strange occurrences, voices, poltergeist activity and visions of a famous actor and actress. In addition, the saloon's stamped tin walls made by Sears and Roebuck are adorned with relics from other southern Nevada boomtowns, including an original Brunswick bar counter from Rhyolite. The Pioneer Saloon is a blast from the past and one of the few remaining saloons of its kind in the United States.

Coincidentally, the must-have menu when visiting this still operational saloon is the Ghost Burger. This burger is mouthwatering and perfectly named for patrons to enjoy when visiting one of the most haunted locations in southern Nevada.

One of the most notable pieces of evidence of the saloon's history is the cigar burns left behind by actor Clark Gable. Gable spent many hours drowning his worries at the bottom of a bottle as he waited for news about his actress wife, Carole Lombard, and her plane crash in nearby Mount Potosi.

In 1942, Lombard was on her way back from a war rally on a flight from Indiana to Los Angeles. The plane refueled in Las Vegas before crashing into Mount Potosi, eleven miles from Goodsprings. Gable sat himself down at the bar of the Pioneer Saloon, waiting to hear back from the search party sent out to look for Lombard's plane. Unfortunately, Gable was not met with good news when the search party returned.

Some say they have seen visions of Gable drinking at the end of the bar, and others have reported seeing Lombard walking through looking for her husband to help console him.

The Pioneer Saloon was where Clark Gable awaited word of the plane crash of his wife, Carole Lombard, in nearby Potosi. *Brian J. Rollins.*

Another one of the famous spirits hanging out at the Pioneer Saloon is that of a gambler, Paul Coski, who was shot after being caught cheating during a game of poker. His shooter was fellow gambler Joe Armstrong, who apparently got into an argument with Coski. Remnants of his murder are visible in the stamped tin walls of the saloon, where patrons can see visible holes left behind by the bullets. To add to the creepiness, a letter from the town's coroner and a newspaper article hang on the wall near the hole, describing how the bullet holes got there.[40]

Some visitors to the Pioneer Saloon have heard the murmurs of saloon activity as if it was softly playing in the background. Sounds of bar excitement, talking, cheering, general chitchat and glasses clinking are heard like they are happening today. The apparition of what is often referred to as "Ruby's Ghost" is spotted hanging out at the bar and wandering just outside the front door. It is unknown who this spirit is, but many believe it was a lady of the night named Ruby who might have worked out of the saloon.

When visiting the Pioneer Saloon, do not be shocked if you find yourself sitting next to an old prospector dressed in old-fashioned mining clothing. This apparition is not afraid to make his appearance known and is often seen sitting at the bar before fading away. Throughout the years, he has been spotted by staff and patrons of the saloon.

Other unexplained occurrences in the bar include loud bangs, strange light anomalies and a sense of dread while sitting at the bar.

Abandoned Miners' Cabins

The community has many of the original mining cabins dating back to the early 1900s. Paranormal researchers have experienced strange temperature readings on the roofs. Some thermal readings were more than a twenty-degree difference in the ninety-degree heat of the Nevada desert.

Inside the cabins, the batteries to paranormal research equipment suddenly get drained, or the devices malfunction. Strange things appear in photos, and unexplainable sounds occur when no one is moving.

It is believed that the oldest cabin in the area—Campbell Cabin —has a dark presence, making anyone who enters feel unwanted.

Goodsprings Schoolhouse

The elementary schoolhouse was built in 1913 and is still being used today, serving the handful of students in Goodsprings. Several stories are being shared around the town claiming several children and a longtime teacher still attend school, even in the afterlife. Paranormal experiences in the schoolhouse include feeling uneasy and being watched by something that does not want anyone in the building. Others have reported seeing apparitions of children and hearing noises similar to that of being in an elementary classroom.

Goodsprings Cemetery

The Goodsprings Cemetery is the final resting place for many residents who have lived and died in the community. This cemetery is one of the more active ones in southern Nevada, with several paranormal investigators

Many leave pennies, nickels, dimes and quarters to pay respect to those buried in the Goodsprings Cemetery. *Brian J. Rollins.*

The Goodsprings Cemetery is the final resting place for many of the town's former residents. *Brian J. Rollins.*

claiming to encounter ghostly figures, experience alien activity and be watched by demonic entities. Some have claimed to encounter red eyes watching them in the darkness only to disappear as they got closer. Several have captured EVPs, seen apparitions, moving mists and bright light anomalies or heard disembodied voices. Plus, the crudely handwritten tombstones and many graves are simple piles of rocks, adding to the creepiness of the cemetery.

WHISKEY PETE'S CASINO PRIMM

Primm, not necessarily a ghost town, is approximately a twenty-minute drive from Goodsprings. Those visiting this small community on the border of Nevada and California have had their share of paranormal activity. Experiences include seeing the apparitions of Whiskey Pete and the infamous Bonnie and Clyde.

Whiskey Pete's Casino is home to a majority of the paranormal activity. Several have encountered Whiskey Pete himself, a former miner and moonshiner in the area. Pete owned a gas station in the area, and when things financially slowed down, he turned to cooking up moonshine in neighboring caves. When Whiskey Pete died, he was buried standing straight up with a glass of whiskey in his hand so he could continue to watch over the area.

His body was accidentally exhumed during the construction of the bridge connecting Whiskey Pete's Casino to Buffalo Bill's Casino over I-15. His remains were relocated to a nearby cave where he created his own moonshine.[41]

Today, there are many reports that Whiskey Pete is overlooking the casino floor, watching everything happening. Others have reported going into the casino and, when returning to their car, discovering they have a full tank of gas when it was near empty before. It is believed that Whiskey Pete is offering a helping hand to those low on gas.

Whiskey Pete's Casino is home to the Bonnie and Clyde death car, in which the outlaw couple, Clyde Barrow and Bonnie Parker, were gunned down in an attempt by U.S. marshals to ensure the couple did not escape. The assault and execution of the couple lasted only twelve seconds but riddled the vehicle with 167 bullets. Each had been shot more than 50 times. The couple's bodies were then pulled into town, still in the car's front seat.[42]

With such a tragic end to their rampage, it is no wonder there might be the energy of Barrow attached to the car. Additionally, Bonnie had wanted the two to be buried together, but her wishes were not met, as their families separated them for their burials. Many have claimed to see Barrow near the death car and feel sorrow when seeing him. Could he be looking for Parker? Or could he be wondering what happened in his final moments? It is unclear why Barrow haunts the car at the casino because the only interaction is catching glimpses of him near the vehicle.

Some visitors have also seen strange light anomalies come out of the car's windows, swoop around and return to the vehicle.

There are definitely some strange occurrences happening in Goodsprings and Primm, making these ghost towns a unique adventure for any paranormal researcher.

CHAPTER 10

JARBIDGE

J arbidge is another ghost town in southern Nevada where the town's tragic history is believed to fuel the paranormal activity. The town was named Jarbidge from the Shoshone language and translates to "devil," "monster that lurks in the canyon" or "weird beastly creature."[43] This name was very fitting, as the Natives believed the nearby hills were haunted and possessed by a demonic being. The so-called devil was from a legend claiming a giant cannibal, Tsawhawbitts, guarded the deep canyon, preventing Native Americans from settling in the area.[44] It was believed the giant roamed the forests collecting unsuspecting souls in a basket to eat.

Stories of strange occurrences in Jarbidge date back to the middle 1880s, when a local ranch worker shared a story about seeing some gold in the hills. His story spread fast, bringing a couple of men on a quest full of trouble and unknown experiences. The two men discovered a cave guarded by a skeleton, which should have been their first warning. Upon entering the cave, both men became extremely ill. Their illness forced them to leave the canyon area for treatment. Unfortunately, one of the men died, and the other never returned or talked about what happened. This unexplainable experience was the beginning of the "Lost Sheepherder Mine" legend.

The hills of the area revealed signs of gold in 1909 to David Bourne, encouraging one of the final gold rushes of the Old West. But like with any boomtown, Jarbidge fell victim to abandonment and an outlaw-inspired community. As most of the residents left town, this out-of-the-way ghost town had only a dirt road leading in and out of town. The isolation and being so far from civilization led this community down a dark path.

On December 5, 1916, a small two-horse mail wagon came to town and was the famous Jarbidge Stage Robbery victim.[45] This mail wagon was an easy target, as it only had the driver, Fred Searcy, protecting the contents. The wagon was ambushed as it headed into town, and the driver was killed. The robbers escaped with more than $4,000, but the driver's killing led residents on a manhunt to capture the perpetrators.

A posse was formed, searching the area for the suspects. Finally, a drifter, Ben Kuhl, and his two friends, Ed Beck and William McGraw, were captured with the .44-caliber pistol believed to be the murder weapon. All three men were taken to Elko for trial and found guilty of their crimes. Kuhl was sentenced and offered a choice of hanging or firing squad. He chose the firing squad and was lucky enough in appeals to get his conviction commuted to life in prison. McGraw served ten months, and Beck served more than six years.

In 1919, the town was almost wiped out when a fire ravaged many multistory buildings and an eatery. In total, twenty-two business establishments and several log cabins were consumed by the fire, including the Success Bar, the telephone office, the dance hall, the movie house and Mrs. McCullock's barbershop.[46]

The Elkoro Mining Company, a branch of Guggenheim's Yukon Gold Company, leased and bought most of the claims in Jarbidge. It ceased operations in the 1930s. When the company left town, it abandoned ninety thousand feet of underground mining operations.

Paranormal explorers visit Jarbidge's claim to see unexplained light anomalies darting through town. The lights appear out of nowhere, fly up in the air and disappear. Some paranormal researchers and visitors to Jarbidge have also reported seeing Bigfoot in the area. But is this creature a Bigfoot, or is it the giant cannibalistic creature Native Americans feared? That question remains unanswered and continues to be researched by many investigators.

CHAPTER 11
POTOSI

According to modern documented history, in 1856, prospecting Mormons in Las Vegas discovered lead ore deposits in a cliff.[47] After this discovery, Nathaniel James came from Salt Lake City to take a look. Upon confirming the mineral deposits, he returned to Utah to get supplies to help develop the mine. Jones named the area Potosi after his boyhood home in Wisconsin. The place started to boom as the Colorado Mining Company set up a smelter at Potosi Spring. Shortly after, many silver mining operations commenced.

In 1905, the San Pedro, Los Angeles and Salt Lake Railroad—now the Union Pacific—was built. The railroad made transporting lead and silver deposits to larger cities easier. In 1910, the Yellow Pine Railroad Outlet was established, and a smelter was built in nearby Goodsprings. Potosi had officially become a top producer of zinc for southern Nevada.

The town was located approximately seven hundred feet below the mine, and one hundred miners made Potosi their home. It is believed that the mine in Potosi was the oldest lode mine in Nevada, with lead deposits discovered in 1847, before the Mormon miners set up camp.

The Empire Zinc Company of New Jersey took over the mine in 1913. The company built extravagant and comfortable homes, which was a significant upgrade from the Mormon log cabins built fifty-eight years earlier. Soon after, an electrical plant and calciner were constructed near the mine, and the excavated ore was quickly transported all over the country.

In 1917, the United States entered World War I, and the government declared Potosi a priority defense project. With its new classification, the mine quickly started producing the zinc, silver and lead the military needed for the war effort.

Potosi was a small mining community and continued operations until 1920. Mining results slowed during the following years, but things picked back up between 1925 and 1928 as the community was extracting lead, silver and zinc from the mines.[48]

The Empire Zinc Company abandoned the Potosi mine, which was then leased to A.J. and A.R Robbins of Goodsprings. After the two took control of the mine, there was another uptick in production. This piqued the interest of the International Smelting Company, which sent engineers to the area to take over the property in 1926. Soon after, Potosi proved that it cost more to mine than it was producing once again.

Several events in Potosi's past could lead to the paranormal activity experienced by those brave enough to explore the area. One possible cause of paranormal activity could be the rumor about the miners using a giant cave in the mountain that the Chemehuevi shaman used for vision quests in the mid-nineteenth century. Or it could be the many miners who lost their lives searching for riches. Maybe the paranormal activity is tied to the TWA Flight 3 that crashed into Potosi Mountain, killing twenty-two passengers, including Lombard, who is believed to haunt nearby at the Pioneer Saloon.[49]

Today, hikers from all over visit Potosi to see the remnants of Lombard's crashed plane. Remarkably enough, more than seventy-five years later, the plane crash site remains on Mount Potosi. Among the debris, explorers have heard voices and cries and had a feeling of not being alone. Does this mean some of the spirits from the plane crash victims still haunt the crash site? Anything's possible.

CHAPTER 12
RIOVILLE

Daniel Bonelli founded the community where the Virgin and the Colorado Rivers meet in 1865. Brigham Young sent him to lead a group of Latter-day Saints to Utah. The group believed they had reached Utah but discovered and set up in what they called Junction City, Nevada. Soon after, the area became a popular destination for steamboats to dock. The site continued to boom until 1887, when silver mining in the region declined.

In 1870, Bonelli purchased Stone's Ferry, renaming it Bonelli's Ferry, and the ferry crossing, and the original residents moved down the river just a few miles away from Junction City. Several years later, new settlers arrived in the area, giving it the name of Rioville. The revived community had a ferry dock and a post office that operated until 1906.

Long before this ghost town was submerged by waters flooding the region in the 1930s with the building of the Hoover Dam, Rioville was nearly abandoned by most of its residents in the late 1890s. Though most of the residents packed up and left during this time, the post office hung in there, and the ferry remained operational until 1934.

Rioville is worth mentioning in this book because it leads some paranormal researchers to wonder if paranormal activity can continue even after a community has been submerged under water. Do the spirits of former residents still go about their business in Rioville? Have they moved to another area? Or is this town even haunted? Unfortunately, because Rioville remains under the waters of Lake Mead, it is nearly impossible to get these answers—at least until researchers develop a better method for underwater investigations.

CHAPTER 13

ST. THOMAS

Another southern Nevada City to succumb to the rising waters of Lake Mead during the construction of the Hoover Dam is St. Thomas. But unlike Rioville, thanks to the lowering water levels of Lake Mead, St. Thomas is now freed from its watery grave.

Long before the original Mormon settlers came to the region, it was inhabited by ancestral Pueblo peoples and the basket makers. Across the river from St. Thomas was an ancestral Puebloan settlement known as the Lost City.

In 1865, St. Thomas was founded as a pioneer settlement, which was primarily quiet, and life passed slowly for those who called the area home.[50] The community served as a stopping point between Salt Lake City and Los Angeles along the Arrowhead Trail. St. Thomas's population rose to about five hundred. All were served by a school, several grocery stores, a post office, a church, a soda fountain shop and several garages to help repair the newly invented automobiles that used the Arrowhead Trail like a modern-day highway.

In 1935, all residents were ordered to leave St. Thomas by the government after it was discovered the waters started to rise during the construction of the Hoover Dam. At the completion of the Hoover Dam, St. Thomas was sixty feet underwater. Hugh Lord packed up his things and paddled away in a canoe in 1938 as the last remaining resident of St. Thomas. It is believed that some residents stood their ground and remained behind. As the waters rose, these remaining residents had nowhere to go and met their demise in the waters of Lake Mead.

It took more than seventy years for the waters to reveal the city once again. Thanks to a significant drought in Nevada, this ghost town is now exposed, waiting to be investigated and researched. With so much death and devastation with the flooding, many spirits may still be left behind to haunt St. Thomas.

When exploring St. Thomas today, many visitors claim to experience uneasy feelings and feel like they are not alone. Shadow people have been seen darting in and out from behind some of the remaining structures that are now visible. Others have reported seeing light anomalies near the ground and over the deserted rubble in the sky. Some have heard voices and cries from the former inhabitants of St. Thomas.

Also, do not be alarmed if sounds of rocks being moved or kicked occur when visiting. It might even be possible to have a rock tossed across pathways as you walk by.

Today, St. Thomas is a shell of its former self. Steps to a ruined home's foundation come up from the ground. Other remnants of buildings dot the landscape, creating an eerie feeling just looking at the devastation left behind by the flooding waters of Lake Mead. All of the structures that have reappeared remind everyone what this town used to be. Will St. Thomas always be available for exploration? For now, it looks possible, but if the waters of Lake Mead were to rise again, St. Tomas might find itself back in its watery prison.

CHAPTER 14

SEARCHLIGHT

Searchlight, like Boulder City, is one former mining town that has revived a bit, keeping it classified just above ghost town status. However, the mining history and rumors of paranormal activity in this town make Searchlight worth mentioning in this book. Several spooky tales involving local bottomless mines and stories claiming the entire town is haunted are shared among residents and paranormal researchers. However, there are not enough substantial claims or corroborating reports on what exactly is haunting this small town.

This town's history could be what fuels that paranormal activity, making it one of the spookiest places to visit. Searchlight's story began when George Colton discovered gold and filed his first claim in 1897 as the Duplex Mine.[51] The following year, a post office was established to support the miners in the camp for the Searchlight Mining District.

Though it is documented when the first claim was discovered, the origins of the town's name have many different versions. Some say it came from a box of Searchlight branded matches used to strike a light when working at night, and others claim it is from the many searchlights used at brothels to capture the attention of potential patrons. Additionally, the town may be named after a riverboat that worked the Colorado River. However, one of the most likely stories regarding how the town was named is when Colton supposedly said, "It would take a searchlight to find gold ore there," just before he discovered gold.

The word about the gold discovery quickly spread, and Searchlight was inundated with miners, leading to the formation of the Quartette Mining Company in 1900. A sixteen-mile narrow-gauge railroad was built to take minerals from the local mines to the company's mill near the Colorado River. Shortly after, in 1902, the town had more than 1,500 residents and was one of the largest and most active mining camps in the area during this time.

The town reached its peak in 1907 with forty-four working mines and more than five thousand residents. Searchlight was home to a telephone exchange and a dozen saloons among the numerous businesses. By 1919, Searchlight was a stop of the Branwell and Searchlight Railroad that connected with the Santa Fe Line to Needles, California. However, by this time, the train was only coming into town twice a week, and the town started to experience the beginning of its decline. Train service ceased in September 1923, when a flood washed out the tracks.

Residents hurriedly packed up and left the area en masse, and by 1927, the town had approximately fifty residents remaining. The mines saw a small spike in productivity in 1934, but it was not enough to keep the town alive. Thanks to the nearby Hoover Dam construction, Searchlight had a slight resurgence in the 1930s and 1940s. The last of the original gold mines officially closed in 1953.

Searchlight is the hometown of Nevada senator Harry Reid, who has become an expert on the town and written several books, including *Searchlight: The Camp that Didn't Fail*.

One of the most mysterious places in Searchlight to explore is the Searchlight Cemetery. Set among the desert landscape and small hillsides, this location has a dead calm atmosphere spooky enough to send chills up any paranormal researcher's spine. Wooden crosses stand crooked, acting like tombstones, sharing little details of who lies beneath. Many of the cemetery plots are outlined in small boulders and rocks, while some have Gothic-looking fences protecting the grave.

Though the cemetery is creepy enough without the spirits haunting the location, some paranormal encounters in the Searchlight Cemetery have occurred there. Visitors have reported seeing strange light anomalies in the cemetery and off in the distance. Additionally, some have encountered shadow figures and heard footsteps when no one else was in the area. Other strange and unexplainable occurrences include the streetlights blinking on and off, especially when trying to communicate with the spirits; feeling watched; and an overwhelming sense of dread.

Another paranormal story circulating among those who have visited and investigated Searchlight is that of a young woman who haunts the town. It is unknown who this woman could be, but she is often seen walking where former graves were located in the central area of the town.

One possible cause of paranormal activity in Searchlight could be from the navy plane that crashed near the town on August 3, 1970.[52] The aircraft was doing a training mission for the Vietnam War from Nellis Air Force Base when it crashed. The Lockheed P-3 Orion was en route to the Barbers Point NAS in Hawaii with a brief stop at North Island–Halsey Field NAS in San Diego. Shortly after takeoff, the aircraft crashed about ten miles northwest of the town, and all ten crew members were killed. It is possible that some of the shadow figures and apparitions spotted throughout Searchlight could be the spirits of the crew of this navy aircraft.

The navy airplane was utterly destroyed, and the debris field extended for more than one-half of a mile. One possible cause of the crash is that the aircraft was struck by lightning after flying through a thunderstorm. However, Lockheed had determined structural overloading of the right wing caused an uncontrollable malfunction, forcing the plane to crash.

Of course, there is a lot of chatter about aliens and UFOs in Nevada, especially with Area 51 a few hours away from Searchlight. There is speculation that the aircraft may have encountered a UFO or was shot down by an alien aircraft. However, official reports claim otherwise, and there is no documented proof to back up the UFO claims.

Today, most of the residents live in mobile homes, leaving many of the original homes and buildings standing in a dilapidated state and wholly abandoned. Due to unethical urban explorers and vandals, little remains in these structures, and many are heavily vandalized.

CHAPTER 15
TONOPAH

As discovered in the earlier pages of this book, Nevada is home to near-endless ghost town opportunities, with many of the locations haunted or having some paranormal claims. For the ghost enthusiast, towns such as Goldfield, Gold Point and Goodsprings allow paranormal researchers to get up close and personal with spirits, entities, aliens and more. Tonopah is one location in Nevada where the spirits enjoy interacting with the living.

After silver was discovered there in May 1900, Tonopah quickly boomed, becoming one of the largest cities in Nevada. Jim Butler is often credited with discovering the first piece of silver ore, which led to the creation of Tonopah.

According to Gary Young's report on October 9, 2014, for KIBS 100.7 FM/1230 AM KBOV Radio, there are three theories regarding Butler and Tonopah.[53] The Burro Legend is the most likely to be true. This legend states that Butler received a tip from local Natives, and he and his burros headed out from his ranch to the Klondike Field. However, while seeking shelter from a severe storm, one of his two burros wandered off.

When he found his burro, it jumped over the ridge, and Butler angrily picked up a stone to throw at the animal. After feeling the weight of the rock, Butler examined it closer and discovered enough silver to take for a sample appraisal. As word traveled quickly about the discovery, Tonopah entered a silver rush.

Abandoned mine and mill, Tonopah, Nevada. *Library of Congress.*

Though there was no mention of a burro in Butler's November 19, 1902 letter to the land registry, this legend continues to be shared as the truth behind the boom.

Paranormal enthusiasts worldwide make their way to Tonopah for the opportunity to experience anything paranormal, and the spirits here do not disappoint. Many who visit Tonopah have opportunities to meet the beautiful and elusive Lady in Red at the Mizpah Hotel or come face to face with George "Devil" Davis at the Tonopah Liquor Company. Ghosts and spirits abound in this ghost town.

According to the official website for Tonopah, it is the place to visit for those who are fascinated by ghosts and have a desire to explore haunted locations.[54]

MIZPAH HOTEL

The Mizpah Hotel in Tonopah opened in 1907, and at the time, local newspapers heralded it as "the finest stone hotel in the desert." The hotel spared no expense, costing more than $200,000 to equip with electric lights, steam heat and a whiskey-stocked bar. It was the vision of United States senator George Nixon and businessmen Cal Brougher, Bob Govan and George Wingfield to establish a high-class hotel where they could conduct their business in the restaurant and bar.[55]

The hotel was constructed on the former Mizpah Saloon and Grill site and designed by architect Morril J. Curtis, who was known for designing the Overland Hotel in Reno and the Grand Opera House. At the time, the Mizpah Hotel was the tallest building in Nevada, with five floors. The hotel's grand opening was hosted on November 17, 1908.

Throughout the years, the hotel became a gathering place for many in the mining and political elite of Nevada, including Tasker Oddie, governor of Nevada; U.S. senator Henry Calvin "Cal" Brougher, the director of the Mizpah Hotel Corporation of Tonopah; and Key Pittman, the state's beloved politician. The hotel was indeed the epicenter of the community for social gatherings and economic activities. Notable guests of the hotel include Wyatt Earp, Tex Rickard and Jack Dempsey.

The hotel has been exquisitely restored by its current owners, Fred and Nancy Cline, who preserved the building's 1907 Victorian style and history. While restoring the hotel to its old characteristics, the couple also managed to add modern comforts and amenities without interfering with the hotel's unique look. For example, the original elevator, the first electric elevator west of the Mississippi, remains in operation, and the Tonopah Banking Corporation's vault is still intact in the hotel's lobby.

Many paranormal researchers, guests and staff of the Mizpah Hotel have claimed to encounter the spirit of a young woman, the Lady in Red.[56] Legends claim she was a woman of the evening offering companionship to travelers in the early 1900s. However, one paranormal report claims she was strangled and stabbed to death by a jealous ex-lover near rooms 501 and 504. A second story about her murder involves her being caught cheating at the hotel by her husband, who strangled her.

Her spirit does not want to move on, as many have sensed her presence and shared ghostly encounters with her spirit. Her spirit enjoys hanging out on the fifth floor and is often seen riding the elevator. Some guests have experienced her leaving them pearls in their room with a sense that she liked them.

Additional reports related to the haunting of the Lady in Red include the sensation of an unseen force touching men's hair or something brushing against their bodies. In addition, some hotel guests have reported smelling a perfume that could be from the 1900s lingering in the halls.

According to the Mizpah Hotel's website, the Lady in Red is not the only spirit haunting the hallways and rooms of the hotel. A group of playful children on the third floor is often heard running up and down the hallways, causing all kinds of noise. Additionally, some guests have reported encountering the spirits of miners who are believed to have been murdered in the basement.

In particular, there is one miner many people claim to have encountered when in the basement. Employees and paranormal researchers have reported unfavorable encounters with a spirit of one miner who is very territorial and angry. The apparition is very tall and slender, wearing traditional miners' clothing.

Could this spirit be that of a murdered miner? If not, what could be causing him to act very territorial over the hotel's basement? Who knows; however, there are very few reports about the spirits in the basement, which leads to much speculation and urban legends. The claims of the angry miner leave one to want to investigate the stories more.

Another legend about the Mizpah Hotel is that of a politician who died in a room on election night. The legend claims his body was kept on ice in the room's bathtub as everyone awaited news of the election results. This legend could explain why some guests have reported seeing the apparition of a man laughing as he stands near the bathtub in their room.

With so many paranormal claims and urban legends surrounding the Mizpah Hotel, there is no wonder why it is considered one of the most haunted places in Nevada.

The Tonopah Liquor Company

An article, "Beyer's Byways: A Night in Tonopah's Haunted Mizpah Hotel,"[57] in the *Daily Press* claims that the Tonopah Liquor Company is home to a spirit named George "Devil" Davis. George appears to be a feisty spirit, playing pranks, which is what he was well known for when alive. Unfortunately, some things don't change in the afterlife.

The Tonopah Liquor Company is also rumored to be haunted by the spirit of a woman named Hattie, who is a very maternal former brothel employee and barmaid. She tends to gravitate toward children and is very kind to them.

Tonopah Historic Mining Park's Visitors' Center

An elegant spirit believed to be Bina Verrault made herself at home in the afterlife at the Tonopah Historic Mining Park's Visitors' Center. Legend claims Verrault was running from the law in New York City and died in Tonopah. Her apparition is spotted peeking out the windows and looking up the hill. In addition, employees of the visitors' center claim to have heard voices and noticed unexplainable activity and movement on security cameras in several areas of the property.

TONOPAH CEMETERY

Cemetery, Tonopah. *Library of Congress.*

Nestled next to the World Famous Clown Motel is the haunted Tonopah Cemetery, founded in 1901. The cemetery was full by 1911 and currently has more bodies than space available, leading Tonopah to find a new plot for burying the dead.

Many gravestones can still be read and share horrific stories of how people perished in this town. Several of the graves were of the miners who died tragically in the Belmont Fire on February 23, 1911, including the burial of Big Bill Murphy, who died trying to save the other miners from the fire. Other gravestones share stories of residents dying from the plague, which was later believed to be an outbreak of pneumonia.

Several strange occurrences are claimed to have happened at these locations, including strange light anomalies, full-bodied apparitions and odd disembodied voices and noises within the cemetery. Spirits of Verrault and Davis may haunt the town, but you can visit their graves at the Tonopah Cemetery.

It is no wonder why many claim the Tonopah Cemetery to be one of Nevada's most unsettling and haunted cemeteries.

THE WORLD FAMOUS CLOWN MOTEL

Those with coulrophobia (the fear of clowns) may not want to venture to Tonopah to visit the World Famous Clown Motel. The hotel is indeed haunted, and the clown theme makes it creepier. In addition, it is located next door to the Tonopah Cemetery, which creates a spooky setting.[58]

Claims of paranormal activity at the Clown Motel include seeing shadow people lurking around corners, disembodied voices and creepy feelings.

The motel's gift shop and museum building have approximately two thousand clown statues, puppets, toys, dolls and art pieces. Some guests claim the spirits are drawn to this building, where most of the paranormal activity occurs.

Out of the thirty-one rooms at the Clown Motel, room 108 is said to be the most active on the property. The room is also referred to as the IT Room, and legend claims an older man passed through Tonopah on his way to have back surgery. However, it is said the man stayed in the room for more than six years until his health drastically declined and an ambulance was called. Unfortunately, the man passed away in the ambulance on the way to Las Vegas; however, many claim he continues to linger in room 108. Paranormal claims in room 108 include an eerie feeling, disembodied voices, strange noises, cold spots and shadow figures.

Vanwood Variety Store

Main Street, Tonopah. *Library of Congress.*

In 1902, Vanwood Variety Store, previously known as the Golden Block, was the first permanent stone building built in Tonopah. The structure was first used as the Nye County Bank, built by Frank Golden, who has a sketchy reputation. Golden was arrested and charged with embezzlement, and some say he haunts the Vanwood Variety Store to this day.

Many employees, shoppers and visitors have reported strange occurrences at the variety shop. Paranormal claims include hearing strange sounds, breezes coming from nowhere, disembodied voices and mysterious light anomalies. It is believed that a former bank employee whom legend claims died in the old safe in the basement is the one causing all the commotion.

Kozy Corner Deli and Coffee Bar

Across the street from the Mizpah Hotel is a quaint location offering unique eats and fresh coffee. Kozy Corner Deli and Coffee Bar is one of the less famous buildings in Tonopah but is one location paranormal enthusiasts must visit.

In an article by Vern Lee in the *Pahrump Valley Times* on October 30, 2013,[59] the owner of Kozy Corner Deli and Coffee Bar, Cori Gonzales, talked about the spirits in her building. She claimed that bread gets thrown, and the bell often rings when no one is near it. Gonzales believes her father is responsible for the paranormal activity in the building built around 1907.

The building was used as a bank and a pharmacy, and Gonzales now rents her space from the Masons upstairs.

CHAPTER 16
BONNIE SPRINGS RANCH

U nfortunately, Bonnie Springs Ranch no longer exists for paranormal researchers or ghost town enthusiasts to visit, study and explore. However, this community built in 1843 is worth mentioning because of the paranormal experiences so many have had when passing through the area. The Paiute Indians initially inhabited the place where Bonnie Springs Ranch was established before being forced out of the region.

Bonnie Springs Ranch was built to serve as a stopover for wagon trains traveling to California along the Old Spanish Trail. This roadside stop was nestled in the heart of Red Rock Canyon in Blue Diamond, Nevada, providing the perfect oasis in the desert for stagecoaches and wagon trains to take a break before continuing to their destination in California.

In 1952, Bonnie McGaugh and Al Levinson saw the potential for the site and set a plan in motion to preserve the area. After a lot of hard work, in 1958, the town was resurrected and opened to the public as a tourist attraction. Before shutting down, Bonnie Springs Ranch served as an attraction providing a Wild West experience, complete with a working saloon, a wedding chapel, shops, a wax museum, restaurants, a replica schoolhouse, daily gunfights and Wild West reenactments. The ranch was also home to a stamp mill, photo gallery, blacksmith's shop, shooting gallery, petting zoo, chapel and opera house. It was an authentic representation of how western life was preserved after many Nevada boomtowns started closing down.

Bonnie Springs Ranch not only provided a recreational outlet for locals and visitors, but it was also one of the most haunted locations in the area, providing those who dared to visit unique stories about supernatural encounters. Paranormal stories from those who visited Bonnie Springs Ranch included the sighting of ghoulish schoolchildren, wax figures coming to life, ghosts lingering in the opera house and apparitions roaming the streets. Some have also reported hearing gunshots in the street, sounds of glasses clinking in the saloon and disembodied voices throughout the ranch. It is possible some of the sounds heard throughout Bonnie Springs Ranch were residual energy, which had been imprinted in the area after years of repetitive activity.

Paranormal activity has been reported in the saloon, opera house, schoolhouse and wax museum. Before it closed, several staff members said they heard footsteps, saw doors slamming and heard other odd sounds. The merry-go-round on the property was often reported as starting to spin independently.

The spirit of a small girl is one of the most commonly told ghost stories shared by those who researched Bonnie Springs Ranch. She was often seen playing around the town's schoolhouse, and when someone approaches, she suddenly disappears. Some believe her playing around is what caused the merry-go-round to move on its own.

Another spooky story from Bonnie Springs Ranch was from the small tunnel-like maze found at the wax museum for those who dared to enter. Some claim that the wax figures in this maze came to life, reaching out to touch them, moving and watching as visitors pass by. Some shared stories that the wax figures looked like they were inhaling and breathing. Employees said management had to secure the mannequins to the floor to prevent them from moving around.

The opera house in Bonnie Springs Ranch was where the most sinister paranormal activity occurred. The menacing presence in the form of a dark shadow figure would follow people around. This figure was captured in photographs by many, and several disturbing EVPs were captured during investigations.

Some believe that era cues can help encourage spirits and make a place more paranormally active. For example, Bonnie Springs Ranch hosted daily gunfights and other reenactments in the community's streets. Could the ghosts have been attracted to this activity? Could they have felt like they were being attacked by a lawless gunslinger and had the need to fight back? Could the paranormal activity be a manifestation of the reenactments and not from former residents? There are so many possibilities that anything is possible. The only thing that paranormal researchers were certain of is that Bonnie Springs Ranch was very active, and it was a sad day when it was sold and set to be demolished.[60]

The ghost town vibe of Bonnie Springs Ranch could have been why so many spirits stayed behind or flocked to the area. It was a place of comfort to them, having everything they had become accustomed to when alive.

CHAPTER 17

More Haunted Southern Nevada Ghost Towns

Not all southern Nevada ghost towns are full of spirits wandering the streets and haunting historic buildings. However, several lesser-known ghost towns still have reports of paranormal activity. These smaller, lesser-known ghost towns simply do not have as many buildings to be haunted, and their past did not have as much death and devastation. Therefore, they have fewer travelers visiting to experience paranormal activity.

This chapter discusses some of those lesser-known ghost towns with reports of paranormal activity.

Berlin

Berlin has all the remnants of an old mining camp that is just calling out to be explored. Because this town is so full of old buildings and other ex– mining town artifacts, it is surprising that Berlin is not among some of the most haunted ghost towns in southern Nevada.

Surprisingly enough, Berlin is home to more than the memories of former mining operations and a wild western life. Instead, this town is home to a sea of undisturbed ichthyosaur fossils, which is just another part of the area's unique history. Many know the area as Berlin-Ichthyosaur State Park, dedicated to protecting the dinosaur fossils and the community's historic mining past.

When walking through the Berlin Historic District, ghost town explorers are surrounded by the remnants of the town's abandoned past. This community has dozens of old structures crumbling right before the eyes. It is a wonder how some of the buildings are still standing because they look so shabby, it almost appears as if nothing is holding them up.

Berlin has a lot of history, and it is waiting to share what life was like to anyone who visits. However, there is a distinctive vibe in the town, and it does not feel like anyone is alone when they walk the streets of this old ghost town.

Berlin, established in 1897 and named after Berlin, Germany, was founded after opening the Berlin Mine, founded the year prior. However, mining in the area has been reported as starting as early as 1862.[61] Once established, Berlin was home to miners, charcoal makers, woodcutters, a forest ranger, a doctor, a nurse and a lady of the night.

In the beginning, residents had high hopes for the town, but it never really experienced the excitement and prosperity many other boomtowns, such as Goldfield, did during this time. Unfortunately, after the turn of the century, Berlin saw a decline, especially after the U.S. financial crisis of 1907, lasting three weeks. The crisis and lack of precious metals being discovered forced many to abandon the town. Berlin had nearly lost all of its residents by 1911.

Luckily for historians and ghost town researchers, the residents left behind plenty of artifacts. Though they are falling apart, many of the original structures provided enough insight into what life was like back when the area was an active mining town. Some of the most well-preserved structures in Berlin include the mine supervisor's home, the machine shop and the assay office. In 1971, the town was finally added to the National Register of Historic Places[62] to help with the town's upkeep and preservation efforts.

Though there are several structures still standing in Berlin, the most impressive is the thirty-stamp mill. Today, it is possible to go inside the structure to look around safely. With the repetitive nature of the stamp mill, many have speculated if it has put a residual imprint on the environment's energy. It is possible because many have heard ghostly sounds of what the stamp mill would have sounded like when visiting Berlin. Several of the town's original residents have been laid to rest in Berlin's cemetery.

Though some have reported seeing the spirits of miners and former residents walk the streets of Berlin, it is not the ghosts that bring people to the town. The Berlin-Ichthyosaur State Park, established in 1957, demonstrates the abundance of prehistoric creatures that once roamed the earth, including the southern Nevada area. This state park was established to display and protect the most extensive known ichthyosaur fossils at the time of its creation. An ichthyosaur is an ancient marine reptile that swam in the warm ocean waters that once covered Nevada more than 225 million years ago.[63] This prehistoric creature ranged in size from two to fifty feet in length.

Luckily, the ghost town of Berlin was included in the park, which helps protect the town and ensures its preservation. In addition to the town being listed in the National Register of Historic Places, the ichthyosaur fossil area is a Registered Natural Landmark. The Berlin-Ichthyosaur State Park encompasses 1,500 acres, providing those seeking a unique adventure filled with history, dinosaurs and ghosts with many exploration opportunities.

COALDALE

Coaldale made its name known when William Groezinger found several deposits of low-grade coal in the area. He sold his claim to Columbia Borax Works in 1894, which had closed until it was reopened and mined again in 1911. In addition to coal, mines in the area produced turquoise and various lesser-valued minerals. Due to the coal discovery in Coaldale[64] and nearby communities, a train station was built to help support the mining efforts in the town. The railroad ran between Sodaville and Coaldale, twenty-five miles, carrying freight and passengers.

Many had high hopes for Coaldale, including Dr. Frances E. Williams, who created a nicely laid out plat full of streets, community parks and other infrastructure items. But unfortunately, these attempts were not enough to keep Coaldale alive. After several disputes and public arguments with a local newspaper, Dr. Williams packed up and left the area, taking every resource she had brought to Coaldale with her.

Since Coaldale turned out to be such a disappointment, many residents left long before the town had a chance to thrive. As a result, the population in this community was always low, with few miners, shop workers, barkeeps and others who worked to provide services and resources for those who attempted to find gold in the nearby hills. By the 1930s, Coaldale primarily served as a rest stop for weary travelers looking for a break, food and fuel. Today, not much remains of Coaldale outside of run-down buildings, destroyed signs, trash and broken glass bottles. The gas station looks like something straight out of an apocalyptic movie. It is overrun by rodents, bugs, weeds and ghosts. The interior and exterior walls of buildings are adorned with graffiti and gang symbols. The abandoned town was the backdrop for the movie *The Stranger* starring Kathy Long.

Due to the hazardous nature of exploring Coaldale and the fact that it was not a thriving mining town, not many paranormal researchers have conducted investigations of this ghost town. Those who have visited this town report strange light anomalies, shadow figures and a feeling of being watched.

MARIETTA

Marietta was a different type of boomtown compared to other mining districts in southern Nevada. This community was built based on the success of the local salt mine, which was more profitable than the silver and gold pulled from neighboring mines.[65] The salt was used to help process silver and gold ore from Virginia City, Aurora and Bodie, Nevada. Later, Marietta started borax mining after a well-known prospector, F.M. "Borax" Smith, helped initiate this new form of mining.

By 1877, Marietta had several hundred residents and several resources, such as saloons, general stores, a post office and mercantiles, to support the workings of the town. However, there was little to no law and order in Marietta because it was one of the most isolated mining camps in southern Nevada. The lawlessness of the camp led to a rowdy lifestyle made up of primarily male bachelors. In 1880, the stage service running in and out of Marietta was robbed thirty times.

This area experienced death, mayhem and traumatic incidents, all of which provide a solid foundation for potential paranormal activity. However, there are no significant reports of ghostly encounters in Marietta, but it is possible to be joined by the spirits of former miners when strolling among the remains in this ghost town.

METROPOLIS

Nestled just north of Wells in Elko County, Nevada, is Metropolis, a ghost town that rose and fell faster than any other boomtown in the area. This town experienced about twenty-five years of success before failing.

During its boom, Metropolis was a wheat farming district founded by the Pacific Reclamation Company of New York and was developed to be the next independent American town. The company installed a water system, a church, schools, saloons, a firehouse and a hotel to help sustain life for the 7,500 residents. This community was also one of the few in Nevada to have concrete sidewalks running throughout.

Metropolis suffered many tragedies during its time, including crops getting destroyed by jackrabbits, a fire devastating the hotel and millions of Mormon crickets invading the city. To top all that off, the area suffered from a drought, which forced farming operations to cease.

No one lives in the town today, but there are approximately seven ranches in the area. The quietness of the town provides an eerie feeling when walking the streets. There are no significant reports of paranormal activity in Metropolis; however, some have reported hearing disembodied voices, seeing shadows and other strange occurrences when visiting the town.

RAWHIDE

The Nevada silver mining industry spread quickly throughout the state's southern portion. With everyone setting their sights on wealth and recognition, many made their way to small towns, such as Rawhide, creating a massive boom in population, amenities and available workers. Unfortunately, thanks to war, the federal government limiting silver in the monetary system and corruption, Rawhide fell victim to the plague of abandoned ghost towns covering Nevada's landscape.[66]

Like many other boomtowns, Rawhide was exposed to the wrongdoings of swindlers and mining promoters who stretched the truth about life in the West in an attempt to draw more people.[67] Everything these hustlers did was to put more money in their pockets at the expense of another's American dream.

One example of a deceptive scheme in towns like Rawhide is how mining promoters would create an extravagant advertisement to entice people to move to the town. Advertising campaigns were the primary reason why Rawhide's population rose swiftly to seven thousand residents. The first official mine location was founded in the town in 1906, and it produced high-grade gold ore. However, Rawhide differed from other boomtowns in southern Nevada because it never really had any mines of significant size.

The town was doing the best it could for being a smaller boomtown. There was a post office, four saloons, two grocery stores, two barbers, two assay offices, two butcher shops and two real estate offices in town. There was also a hotel, a lodging house, three banks and schoolhouses, and several lots were divided up for private residences for the miners and workers. Residents had plenty of resources to enjoy life among the southern Nevada landscape.[68]

Unfortunately, Rawhide suffered a large fire on September 4, 1908, which destroyed a significant portion of the business area of the town. In addition, the fire caused several hundreds of dollars in damage to the town. Then, the following year, the town was affected by a flood. Plus, during this time, claim jumpers attempted to steal mining claims, and bandits ran amuck, robbing miners, residents and desert travelers.

It's sad to say from a paranormal researcher's perspective that a small town with so much con-artistry, swindling, death, chaos and mayhem does not have any significant reports of paranormal activity. Is it possibly because Rawhide is not often visited because it is out of the way, and no one is there to experience any interactions with spirits? Or is it that all the spirits from Rawhide have moved on? Either way, it would be interesting to see if anything paranormal still lingers in this out-of-the-way boomtown.

SOUTHERN NEVADA IS HOME to many ghost towns, some more well known than others. It is not uncommon to come across a ghost town and wonder about the history and if any spirits remain there. Other ghost towns in southern Nevada include those in Nye, Lincoln, Mineral, Clark and Esmeralda Counties.

The Reduction Mill around 1871 in Bullionville, Nevada. *Library of Congress.*

Ghost towns found throughout southern Nevada include Alturas, Belleville, Blair, Bristol Wells, Broken Hills, Bullionville, Cactus Springs, Callville, Candelaria, Colorado City, Columbus, Crystal Springs, Currant, Delamar, Eagleville, Fish Lake Valley, Gold Center, Grantsville, Hiko, Ione, Johnnie, Logan, Louisville, Lucky Jim Camp, Midas, Miller's, Mountain City, Palmetto, Pioneer, San Juan, Silver Canyon, Simonsville, St. Joseph, Tempiute, Tybo and Ute.

Several of the remaining ghost towns are easy to get to, with roads going in and out of the town. Some are working ghost towns with tours, restaurants, shops and hotels. However, other ghost towns are not as easy to get to. Some require extensive hiking skills or can only be reached by ATV.

Regardless of the status, all of the ghost towns in southern Nevada helped make this region what it is today—an exciting place to explore, with many unique opportunities to encounter something paranormal.

Notes

Chapter 1

1. Lexico Dictionaries, "GHOST TOWN English Definition."
2. Hall, *Ghost Towns and Mining Camps*, 6, 7.
3. Nevada National Security Site, "About the NNSS."
4. Clark County, "Clark County Museum."

Chapter 2

5. Legends of America, "Tommyknockers."

Chapter 3

6. National Park Service, "Rhyolite Ghost Town."
7. Utah State University, "Bottle House of Rhyolite."
8. Moffat, *Memoirs*, 3.
9. Goldwell Museum.
10. Aliens Latest, "Google Earth User Discovers 'Creepy Men Standing in a Circle.'"
11. Leong, "Historic Nevada Brothel for Sale."
12. Western Mining History, "Montgomery-Shoshone Mine."

Chapter 4

13. Western Mining History, "Belmont Nevada."
14. Hufman, "Charles Manson, Belmont and a Woman Named Rose."

Chapter 5

15. Boulder City Pet Cemetery.
16. Places That Were, "Hospital of the Damned."
17. Bureau of Reclamation, "Hoover Dam: Fatalities at Hoover Dam."
18. Boulder City, "Is the Boulder Dam Hotel Haunted?"
19. *Boulder City Review*, "Picture Captures Final Moments of Woman's Life."
20. *Los Angeles Times*, "Two Die in Hughes' Test Flight Crash."
21. National Park Service, "Historic Lake Mead B-29."
22. Light in the Dark Place, "Plans of the Satanic NWO Exposed!"
23. Bureau of Reclamation, "Hoover Dam: Dog on a Catwalk."

Chapter 6

24. tubi, "Real Haunts: Ghost Towns."
25. *The Sun*, "Inside Creepy Abandoned Mining Town."
26. Nelson Ghost Town, "Photography, Tours, & Weddings."

Chapter 7

27. Gold Point Ghost Town, "VACATION in the OLD WEST in a Real Live Ghost Town!"
28. MSN, "See How Many UFO Sightings Have Occurred in Nevada."

Chapter 8

29. Western Mining History, "Goldfield Nevada."
30. *Sea Coast Echo*.
31. Esmeralda County, Nevada, "Goldfield, Nevada."

Bibliography

Aliens Latest. "Google Earth User Discovers 'Creepy Men Standing in a Circle' in Deserted Ghost Town—Goldwell Open Air Museum." October 3, 2021. news-intel.com/goldwell-open-air-museum.

Aurich, Jon. Review of the Florence Mine, interview by Heather Leigh Carroll-Landon. 2020.

Beyer, John R. "Beyer's Byways: A Night in Tonopah's Haunted Mizpah Hotel." *Daily Press*, October 17, 2021. www.vvdailypress.com/story/lifestyle/travel/2021/10/17/beyers-byways-night-tonopahs-haunted-mizpah-hotel/8467116002.

Boardman, Mark. "The Last Stage Robbery?" *True West Magazine*, November 1, 2016. truewestmagazine.com/last-stage-robbery.

Boulder City: Home of Hoover Dam and Lake Mead. "Is the Boulder Dam Hotel Haunted?" www.bouldercity.com/is-the-boulder-dam-hotel-haunted.

Boulder City Pet Cemetery. www.bouldercitypetcemetery.org.

Boulder City Review. "Picture Captures Final Moments of Woman's Life." January 16, 2014. bouldercityreview.com/news/lake-mead-hoover-dam/picture-captures-final-moments-of-womans-life.

Bureau of Aircraft Accidents Archives. "Crash of a Lockheed P-3A-55-LO Orion Near Searchlight: 10 Killed." www.baaa-acro.com/crash/crash-lockheed-p-3a-55-lo-orion-near-searchlight-10-killed.

Bureau of Reclamation. "Hoover Dam: Dog on a Catwalk." usbr.gov/lc/hooverdam/history/articles/dog.html.

—————. "Hoover Dam: Fatalities at Hoover Dam." www.usbr.gov/lc/hooverdam/history/essays/fatal.html.

Clark County, Nevada. "Clark County Museum." www.clarkcountynv.gov/government/departments/parks___recreation/cultural_division/musuems/clark_county_museum.php.

Esmeralda County, Nevada. "Goldfield, Nevada." www.accessesmeralda.com/communities/goldfield.php.

Eureka [NV] Sentinel. September 20, 1913. chroniclingamerica.loc.gov/lccn/sn86076201/1913-09-20/ed-1/seq-4.

Find a Grave. "Whiskey Pete's Grave in Primm, Nevada." www.findagrave.com/cemetery/2425544/whiskey-petes-grave.

Forgotten Nevada. "Coaldale." forgottennevada.org/sites/coaldale.html.

—————. "Marietta." www.forgottennevada.org/sites/marietta.html.

—————. "Rawhide." www.forgottennevada.org/sites/rawhide.html.

Ghost Towns. "Potosi." www.ghosttowns.com/states/nv/potosi.html.

—————. "Rawhide." ghosttowns.com/states/nv/rawhide.html.

Goldfield Historical Society. "The Florence Mine." www.goldfieldhistoricalsociety.com/the-florence-mine.

—————. "John S. Cook." goldfieldhistoricalsociety.com/featured-johnscook.html.

—————. "Virgil Walter Earp in Goldfield." www.goldfieldhistoricalsociety.com/virgil-walter-earp-in-goldfield.

Gold Point Ghost Town. "VACATION in the OLD WEST in a Real Live Ghost Town!—Located in Goldpoint, Nevada." www.goldpointghosttown.com.

Goldwell Museum. www.goldwellmuseum.org.

Hall, Shawn. *Ghost Towns and Mining Camps of Southern Nevada.* Charleston, SC: Arcadia Publishing, 2010.

Haunted Hotels of America. "Mizpah Hotel." www.historichotels.org/us/hotels-resorts/mizpah-hotel.

Hee, Vern. "Ghost Hunting 101: Tonopah's Tiniest Ghost Hunter Gets Lesson from Pros." *Pahrump Valley Times*, October 30, 2013. pvtimes.com/news/ghost-hunting-101-tonopahs-tiniest-ghost-hunter-gets-lesson-from-pros.

Howard Hickson's Histories. "Jarbidge, Nevada." www.gbcnv.edu/hickson/Jarbidge2.html.

Hufman, Matt. "Charles Manson, Belmont and a Woman Named Rose." *Las Vegas Sun*, September 18, 2013. lasvegassun.com/features/finding-nevada/2013/sep/18/charles-manson-belmont-and-woman-named-rose.

Lasky, Jacob. "The 7 Most Haunted Places in Las Vegas." *Vegas News*, October 8, 2021. www.vegasnews.com/212625/the-7-most-haunted-places-in-las-vegas.html.

Legends of America. "Searchlight, Nevada Lives On." www.legendsofamerica.com/nv-searchlight.

———. "Tommyknockers of the Western Mines." www.legendsofamerica.com/gh-tommyknockers.

Leong, Grace. "Historic Nevada Brothel for Sale." *Las Vegas Sun*, September 21, 2000. lasvegassun.com/news/2000/sep/21/historic-nevada-brothel-for-sale.

Lexico Dictionaries | English. "GHOST TOWN English Definition and Meaning." www.lexico.com/en/definition/ghost_town.

The Light in the Dark Place. "Plans of the Satanic NWO Exposed! The Hoover Dam Plaque, Bud Light Ad and the Gods of Egypt." www.thelightinthedarkplace.com/plans-of-satanic-nwo-exposed-hoover-dam.

Los Angeles Times. "Two Die in Hughes' Test Flight Crash." May 16, 2006. www.latimes.com/archives/la-xpm-2006-may-16-me-a2anniversary16-story.html.

Lovelock [NV] Tribune. December 21, 1906. chroniclingamerica.loc.gov/lccn/sn86091313/1906-12-21/ed-1/seq-4.

Lundeberg, Cyndi. "Bonnie Springs Ranch Set to Be Demolished in March." FOX5 Las Vegas. www.fox5vegas.com/news/bonnie-springs-ranch-set-to-be-demolished-in-march/article_0b9d7bf0-1473-11e9-b876-83925392a57c.html.

Mizpah Hotel. "Jewel of the Desert." www.themizpahhotel.com.

Moffat, James R. *Memoirs of an Old-Timer: Rhyolite, Nevada 1906–1907*. N.p.: Sage Brush Press, 1963, 3.

MSN. "See How Many UFO Sightings Have Occurred in Nevada." www.msn.com/en-us/news/technology/see-how-many-ufo-sightings-have-occurred-in-nevada/ar-AAS1pU7.

National Park Service. "Historic Lake Mead B-29—Lake Mead National Recreation Area." www.nps.gov/lake/learn/historic-lake-mead-b-29.htm.

———. "Rhyolite Ghost Town—Death Valley National Park." www.nps.gov/deva/learn/historyculture/rhyolite-ghost-town.htm.

———. "St. Thomas Nevada—Lake Mead National Recreation Area." www.nps.gov/lake/learn/nature/st-thomas-nevada.htm.

Nelson Ghost Town. "Photography, Tours, & Weddings." nelsonghosttown.com.

Nesbitt, Mark, and Katherine M. Ramsland. *Blood & Ghosts: Paranormal Forensic Investigations*. Gettysburg, PA: Second Chance Publications, 2012.

Nevada Ghost Town. "Jarbidge." ghosttowns.com/states/nv/jarbidge.html.

Nevada Magazine. "Yesterday: Potosi Mine." nevadamagazine.com/issue/july-august-2019/10367.

Nevada Mining Association. "Nevada Ghost Towns: Rawhide." www.nevadamining.org/rawhide-nevada.

Nevada National Security Site. "About the NNSS." www.nnss.gov/pages/about.html.

Nevada Public Radio. "75 Years Later: Carole Lombard and the Crash into Mt. Potosi." knpr.org/knpr/2017-01/75-years-later-carole-lombard-and-crash-mt-potosi.

Nevada State Parks. "Berlin-Ichthyosaur State Historic Park | State Parks." parks.nv.gov/parks/berlin-ichthyosaur.

Perth Amboy [NJ] Evening News. July 7, 1923. chroniclingamerica.loc.gov/lccn/sn85035720/1923-07-07/ed-2/seq-10.

Places That Were. "Hospital of the Damned." www.placesthatwere.com/2016/04/hospital-of-dammed.html.

Rollins, Brian J. Review of paranormal experiences, interview by Heather Leigh Carroll-Landon, 2022.

ROUTE Magazine. "The Ghosts of the Goldfield Hotel." www.routemagazine.us/stories/the-ghosts-of-the-goldfield-hotel.

Sea Coast Echo (Bay St. Louis, MS). January 6, 1906. chroniclingamerica.loc.gov/lccn/sn86074033/1906-01-06/ed-1/seq-5.

State Historic Preservation Office. "Nevada's Historic Places." shpo.nv.gov/state-and-national-registers.

The Sun. "Inside Creepy Abandoned Mining Town That Bears Scars of Epic Hollywood Scene." December 22, 2016. www.thesun.co.uk/news/2458064/abandoned-american-ghost-town-pictures-3000-miles-to-graceland.

Tonopah, Nevada. "Haunted Tonopah." www.tonopahnevada.com/haunted-tonopah.

Travel Nevada. "Partial to the Pioneer Saloon." March 28, 2015. travelnevada.com/bars/partial-to-the-pioneer-saloon.

tubi. "Real Haunts: Ghost Towns." tubitv.com/movies/603709/real_haunts_ghost_towns.

Utah State University. "The Bottle House of Rhyolite—Graveyard of Dreams: The Story of Aurora and Rhyolite—USU Digital Exhibits." exhibits.usu.edu/exhibits/show/rhyolitedreams/building-rhyolite/bottlehouse.

Western Mining History. "Belmont Nevada." westernmininghistory.com/towns/nevada/belmont.

———. "Berlin Nevada." westernmininghistory.com/towns/nevada/berlin.

———. "Florence Mine." westernmininghistory.com/mine-detail/10046708.

———. "Goldfield Nevada." westernmininghistory.com/towns/nevada/goldfield.

———. "Jarbidge Nevada." westernmininghistory.com/towns/nevada/jarbidge.

———. "Montgomery-Shoshone Mine." westernmininghistory.com/mine_detail/10044475.

Williamson, Brian. Review of paranormal encounters, interview by Heather Leigh Carroll-Landon, 2022.

The World Famous Clown Motel. www.theclownmotelusa.com.

Young, Gary. "Jim Butler & the Discovery of Tonopah, Nevada." KIBS 100.7 FM/1230 AM KBOV, October 9, 2014. www.kibskbov.com/2014/10/jim-butler-discovery-of-tonopah.

About the Author

Heather Leigh Carroll-Landon, PhD, started her journey in the paranormal field as a teenager after multiple interactions with her grandfather, who passed away many years prior. She has researched and traveled to locations throughout the years following to learn more about history and paranormal claims. As long as she has been interested in the supernatural, Heather Leigh has been a freelance writer, writing for several newspapers, magazines and online publications.

She holds a doctorate of philosophy in metaphysical and humanistic science specializing in paranormal science. She is a certified paranormal investigator and a certified EVP technician. Her goal is to help others take a more scientific approach to paranormal investigations and research.

Heather Leigh is the chief administrator for The Warren Legacy Foundation for Paranormal Research and a ParaNexus Anomalous Research Association member. She and her family appeared in *Real Haunts: Ghost Towns* and *Real Haunts 3*, where they explored many of the southern Nevada ghost towns you discovered in this book.

She is an author of articles and books and a lecturer about all things paranormal. She is a co-host and content contributor for *Touch of Magick*, a podcast about magick and the supernatural, and teaches classes through iMystic University. Heather Leigh is also the founder of Exploration Paranormal and co-founder of Witches Paranormal Society. She also co-hosts *The Warren Files* and *Ghost Education 101* vodcasts on Facebook and is the host of *Exploring the Paranormal* vodcast, also on Facebook.

You can find Heather Leigh on Facebook @DrHeatherLeigh, where you will find additional information, including upcoming classes, lectures and more.

Visit us at
www.historypress.com